The Global Education Race

The Global Education Race

Taking the Measure of PISA and International Testing

SAM SELLAR
Department of Childhood, Youth and Education Studies, Manchester Metropolitan University

GREG THOMPSON
Faculty of Education, Queensland University of Technology

DAVID RUTKOWSKI
Centre for Educational Measurement, University of Oslo

Brush Education Inc.
www.brusheducation.ca
contact@brusheducation.ca

Cover design: Dean Pickup; Cover images: iStock: FatCamera
Interior design and layout: Carol Dragich, Dragich Design

Library and Archives Canada Cataloguing in Publication

Sellar, Sam, author
    The global education race : taking the measure of PISA and international testing / Sam Sellar (Department of Childhood, Youth and Education Studies, Manchester Metropolitan University), Greg Thompson (Faculty of Education, Queensland University of Technology), David Rutkowski (Centre for Educational Measurement, University of Oslo).

Includes bibliographical references and index.
Issued in print and electronic formats.
ISBN 978-1-55059-711-0 (softcover).—ISBN 978-1-55059-712-7 (PDF).—
ISBN 978-1-55059-713-4 (Kindle).—ISBN 978-1-55059-715-8 (EPUB)

    1. Programme for International Student Assessment. 2. Educational tests and measurements—Methodology. 3. Educational tests and measurements--Cross-cultural studies. 4. Educational evaluation—Cross-cultural studies. 5. Academic achievement—Cross-cultural studies. I. Thompson, Greg, 1973-, author II. Rutkowski, David, author III. Title.

LB3051.S45 2017   371.26   C2017-901369-6
                                                      C2017-901370-X

Contents

Foreword: PISA—A good servant but a bad master   vii
David C. Berliner and Pasi Sahlberg

Acknowledgements   xiii

Introduction: Running the wrong race?   1

1 The PISA Racetrack   5

2 Stories   17

3 Rankings   27

4 Tests   41

5 Comparisons   55

6 Validity   69

7 Politics   83

Conclusion: Helping policy-makers find the right track   95

References   101
About the Authors   105

PISA: A good servant but a bad master

We believe there is widespread agreement that the world is flatter, more interconnected than ever before, and that in such a world, those with a better education will find employment quicker and at higher salaries than those with worse education. Thus it is natural for citizens and public figures to ask how they might determine if their nation (or province or state) meets the needs of their youth so that they can thrive in an age of globalization of workforces and intense international competitiveness.

Over the last few decades, the answer that has been promoted to that question has been for nations to engage in large-scale international student assessments. These assessments seek to find Global Learning Metrics (GLMs) to help nations evaluate their own educational systems against those of others and to aid in a search for best practices with which to improve their systems. Having such GLMs would be wonderful, but of course they would have to be fair to all nations. They would have to assess students in all nations at the same age and grade, and they would have to be sure that questions presented in Greek, Finnish, English, French, and other languages were interpreted the same way in each nation; that pictures and problem contexts for questions were interpreted the same way in each nation; that the samples of students drawn in each nation yielded students for testing that were highly comparable; that the nature of test preparation for a particular GLM was relatively equal; and so forth. If this sounds like an impossible task, you have figured out the fundamental problem in developing valid GLMs for comparing national or sub-national systems of education.

The Programme for International Student Assessment (PISA) is the best known of the international assessments attempting to provide GLMs. On top of the problems of all international assessments already noted, PISA has three additional problems. First, PISA attempts to predict the quality of the workforce and the future competitiveness of a nation's economy from the test scores of 15-year-old students in school during the year of testing. That too seems impossible to do well since no tests we know of predict something as complex as economic growth and a nation's economic performance over long periods of time. It is also telling that currently there is no strong association between national economic competitiveness and students' performance in PISA.

Second, we know that throughout much of the world, the scores on standardized achievement tests are much less a function of the schools students attend and much more a function of the social conditions and income levels of the students who attend those schools. So scores on PISA tests are much more highly linked to the social conditions affecting the children of each nation than they are to that nation's school system.

Third, education systems around the world have begun to value and privilege reading, mathematical, and scientific literacies more than other subjects or themes in their curricula. This trend had already started before PISA was used for the first time, but it has been reinforced in all the nations competing in PISA. Nevertheless, there are many other things in school that children need to learn in order to be "well educated" and succeed in life. It is evident to us that in the United States, for example, civics, arts, music, and physical activity have been the victims of curricular transitions in schools. PISA has affected other national education systems in similar ways. When the race to the top gets tougher, we find everywhere we have looked in recent years that curriculum narrows and children suffer.

Because of our many concerns about the problems with GLMs, we are delighted to introduce readers to this timely and clearly written book. It is outstanding in its factual base and the clarity of its writing. It informs and warns, but it is neither anti-testing nor anti-PISA. In fact, the authors note that PISA has been carefully prepared and well documented, so the scholarly community can thoroughly examine test development and the analyses that follow. But what these authors ask for, and what we applaud them for, is that interpretations of PISA be more modest than those provided by many news reporters and ministers of education. All tests have limitations. Numbers do not have the objectivity sometimes ascribed to them. In a world that seems to value metrics, however derived, over human judgment, PISA may be one of a number of assessments that is overly valued for the information it can provide. PISA scores certainly do not have the talismanic properties often ascribed to them!

The authors point out that PISA has been very successful in influencing educational discourse, though its results have not always been interpreted appropriately, and decisions based on those scores have not always improved an educational system. It turns out that the effects of PISA have not always been benign! For example, a nation falling in rank from 5th to 10th or rising in rank from 15th to 10th has barely changed in raw scores at all. But because PISA reports ranks, making educational systems compete as if in a horse race, national hysteria or euphoria may follow the release of such information. Nations always feel the need to win, not lose, the races in which they compete. But when ranks are used, there is only one winner and a lot of unhappy national leaders. Politicians and journalists often forget that the many inferences offered to explain changes in a nation's scores over time are almost impossible to verify. Scores do change, but the reasons they do so are devilishly hard to substantiate.

This important book also addresses another aspect of PISA and other international large-scale assessments when they are used as a criterion for global benchmarking in education. The OECD's own analysis and several studies about how PISA affects national education policies and policy-making processes suggest that most of the 35 OECD member countries have changed their educational strategies in one way or another because of their participation in PISA. Extreme examples of mistaken goals abound, such as when national education policy targets are set by aiming at achieving a certain rank in international league tables (e.g., being among the top five education systems by 2025). Equally harmful is when PISA is the cause of a shift of human and other resources from "less important" areas of schooling to those subjects that are measured in PISA.

Furthermore, all student assessments that have high stakes attached to them are always subject to cheating, misuse, and systemic corruption. PISA, with its increasingly high political significance to politicians and governments, is no exception. Donald Campbell phrased his well-known law in his 1975 article by saying, "the more any quantitative social indicator is used for social decision-making, the more subject it will be to corruption pressures and the more apt it will be to distort and corrupt the social processes it is intended to monitor." We think Campbell is right. Research has shown that wrongdoings almost always manifest themselves when a test takes on too much significance. Although the authors don't refer to possible threats to integrity when describing the usage and implications of PISA, we would like to remind readers that regardless of safeguards and carefully controlled protocols for administering PISA, like any other high-stakes quantitative social indicator, PISA is a potential target of unethical policies and practices.

The authors do rightly note that when governments use standardized testing as a tool to manage and control teacher practice and performance, they quickly run into problems. The authors' vision, like ours, is quite different. They call for informed, critical engagement with testing by both the public and a nation's political leaders in order to improve the quality of the data generated and also to support the use of data in valid ways. Obviously this calls for a higher level of assessment literacy than now exists in education, among the public, or among political leaders and journalists. In our age of metrification, deeper understanding of the metrics influencing lives across the globe is certainly needed, and this book is a wise and lucid introduction to why that is so.

David C. Berliner & Pasi Sahlberg

REFERENCE

Campbell, D. T. (1975). Assessing the impact of planned social change. In G. Lyons (Ed.), *Social research and public policies: The Dartmouth/ OECD Conference.* (Chapter 1, pp 3-45). Hanover, NH: Dartmouth College, The Public Affairs Center. (p. 35).

David C. Berliner is Regents' Professor of Education Emeritus at Arizona State University. He is a member of the National Academy of Education, the International Academy of Education, and a past president of both the American Educational Research Association (AERA) and the Division of Educational Psychology of the American Psychological Association (APA).

Pasi Sahlberg is the author of the bestseller *Finnish Lessons 2.0: What Can the World Learn from Educational Change in Finland?* (Teachers College Press, 2015) and numerous professional articles and book chapters. He is former Director General of CIMO (Centre for International Mobility and Cooperation) at Finland's Ministry of Education and Culture in Helsinki and a visiting Professor of Practice at Harvard University's Graduate School of Education in Cambridge.

Acknowledgements

This book emerged from a series of conversations between the authors and groups of educators across Canada. Over the past few years, the Alberta Teachers' Association (ATA), including its research unit, has made it possible for us to share and develop our ideas about international testing and schooling by engaging with teachers, school leaders, fellow academics, and staff from teacher organizations. This book reflects some of the many things we have learned from these conversations and will realize the ATA's goal of advancing more informed public debates about how to achieve great schools for all students in Canada and the rest of the world.

Running the wrong race?

October 2013, Toronto. Sam, one author of this book, was late. He had a plane to catch and had just discovered that the Toronto Marathon was going to complicate the journey. The hotel concierge explained that the race was causing traffic jams and a taxi would not get him to the city airport on time. He needed to take the subway from Museum to Union and then transfer to a bus. He checked Google Maps and committed the directions to memory. Sam had visited Toronto several times and felt confident navigating the subway and downtown area. The problem was time; he had to be quick.

It felt like an eternity waiting for the train, but it arrived on schedule and he was soon disembarking into busy Union station. But which exit did he need? He headed for Front Street but unwittingly found himself on the wrong corner. He followed the directions in his head, but he was starting from the wrong place and ended up trying to board a bus for the wrong airport. The driver pointed out his error but knew nothing about the bus he needed. He consulted Google Maps again and found his way to the correct corner. There was no bus. Time was running out. He decided to walk.

Well, it was actually more like a half-walk, half-run, tending more and more toward the latter as he realized just how far he had to go to reach the ferry terminal for the airport, which is located on an island in Lake Ontario. As he headed toward the waterfront, he could see the crowds lining the marathon course. Making his way through the spectators, he had a sinking feeling as he realized they were cheering runners along Lake Shore Boulevard. He needed to cross Lake Shore Boulevard.

Nearly 3,600 people completed the marathon that day, and it seemed that most were currently snaking along this part of the course in a human stream that was 15 people deep. The imminently departing ferry was visible in the distance. As he was sizing up his prospects for crossing the runners, someone offered advice: "The only way to cross safely is to run in the same direction and zigzag to the other side." The image of Frogger, a popular 1980s arcade game, immediately came to mind. The airport was a few hundred metres ahead and slightly to the right. The runners were heading left. He picked up his suitcase and began running with them and through them. He had joined a race he did not want to be in, and he was running in the wrong direction from his goal.

The ferry departed as Sam was making his way back toward the terminal. Years later he discovered there was also a pedestrian tunnel that he could have taken. It turned out that this was actually the most important piece of information. But at the time, he was so consumed with reaching his destination as quickly as possible that he didn't explore alternatives. Sam missed the boat, and he also missed his plane.

When we find ourselves in a race, we can become overwhelmed by the urgency of getting ahead without pausing to consider where we are going. This can result in a situation brilliantly illustrated by Monty Python's famous Silly Olympics event: the 100-metre dash for people with no sense of direction. The runners assemble at the starting line after anxious preparations, the starting pistol is fired, and the runners veer off in all directions. No one heads toward the finish line and the commentator remarks, "Well, that was fun, wasn't it?"

It has become common to hear talk of a "global education race" that pits countries and school systems against one another. Fear of being left behind in this race now haunts policy-makers and school leaders around the world. Even though most of them did not choose to join the race, it is easy to be swept up in the urgency of getting ahead. The risk is that school systems may find themselves running in the wrong direction in pursuit of reforms that will not get them where they need to go. Having the right information is crucial. This short book provides key information about the global education race and international testing that will help educators consider where they should be going and whether racing is the best way to get there.

1

The PISA Racetrack

1.1 Fear of falling behind

If you ask a group of school teachers who has the world's leading education system, it is a safe bet that many would suggest Finland or somewhere in East Asia. Others would proudly nominate their own school system. But if you ask the same teachers to raise their hand if they have heard of PISA, then you might see about half of the group with hands in the air. If you ask what the acronym stands for, then few hands would remain raised (it stands for the Programme for International Student Assessment). People are familiar with stories of educational success and failure but are not always sure where the stories come from.

In late 2010, a flurry of newspaper headlines proclaimed that Shanghai had the smartest students in the world and other systems were in danger of being left behind in the "global education race." For example, the *New York Times* announced on 7 December 2010 that "Top test scores from Shanghai stun educators." The article quoted President Obama as saying that the United States was experiencing a new "Sputnik moment" and had to face the challenge of catching up to East Asian school systems. The *Globe and Mail* published an article explaining "How Canada is becoming outclassed in school" (8 December 2010). Headlines in other countries, such as England and Australia, also drew attention to the strong performance of Shanghai and expressed a fear that school systems in their own countries were falling behind.

Stories about educational crises capture attention and promote a sense that change of some kind is urgently required. For example, in the early 1980s, the report *A Nation at Risk* warned that American schools were falling behind other nations in mathematics and science performance; this narrative still has effects today. In 2001, Germany experienced an educational crisis when it placed 22nd in the world for student performance in reading. In 2003, debate was sparked in Japan when the reading literacy of its students was ranked 14th in the world. In 2013, commentators across Canada announced that the country had a mathematics crisis after performance fell significantly in most provinces. We could add many other examples to this list.

But how do we know that students in Shanghai are running ahead of students in the United States? How did Germany discover that it placed 22nd in the world for reading? How does Canada know whether it is falling behind in mathematics? The answer to each of these questions is PISA. While many educators do not know much about PISA itself, it has become the main track on which the global education race is run.

PISA is an international large-scale assessment of educational performance conducted by the Organisation for Economic Co-operation and Development (OECD). When we read headlines comparing educational performance in one country against others, it is likely that the story started from PISA. But while PISA has arguably become the most influential educational assessment today, many classroom teachers and parents have either not heard of it or know very little about it. This makes sense because PISA does not have a direct impact on students, teachers' work, or life in schools more generally. However, PISA does shape thinking about education around the world, and the results are used as evidence to justify reforms and interventions that can have far-reaching consequences. This book has been written for educators, parents, and other education stakeholders who may know little about PISA, but who indirectly experience its effects as the assessment reshapes education policy, public debate, and everyday life in classrooms and schools.

1.2 Aims of this book

This book has been written to help people understand what PISA is, what it does, and what it cannot do. Why is such a book needed? The academic literature on PISA has grown dramatically since the assessment was first conducted in 2000 and, along with the newspaper headlines it generates, there has also been a proliferation of commentary on PISA in the form of blog posts, tweets, protest letters, and so on. Much has been written about PISA, offering technical analysis, polemical critique, or uncritical acceptance of the results as exposing educational success or crises. What is still needed is an accessible introduction that enables people (1) to understand how PISA shapes educational thinking and practice and (2) to join the debate about PISA from an informed position. This book aims to meet these needs and to challenge some myths and fallacies about the performance and comparison of school systems that have emerged with the growing influence of PISA.

This is not an anti-testing book.

We are currently witnessing a dramatic growth in the use of data to monitor and evaluate almost every aspect of our daily lives. Facebook now understands who we are better than close relatives, and Target is better than we are at predicting what we need. We are riding a wave of "datafication" that not only looks unlikely to recede, but may also bring many benefits, such as increasing our understanding and improving our decision making in a variety of contexts. Of course, these developments also create new risks and controversies, which is why it is important to understand how data shape our lives.

As politicians and policy-makers need to understand and make decisions about complex education systems, there is likely to be growing demand for new kinds of data analytics that make things simpler. While those who oversee large education systems might be moved by stories about how a particular school turned around the learning of one child who had trouble with reading, these stories do not help them make decisions about where to spend their limited budgets or how to intervene if the system is not giving all students a fair chance. While recent movements to reduce or opt-out of standardized testing have had success in some jurisdictions, it is difficult to imagine education systems completely rejecting standardized testing. Rather than opposing testing in principle, we favour a pragmatic approach to understanding how educational testing works and how it might be improved. This pragmatic approach requires that teachers, parents, and other education stakeholders be supported to engage with testing in meaningful and insightful ways.

This is not an anti-PISA book.

Governments make use of PISA in many ways, and it is not the aim of this book to argue that PISA, or the OECD's education data more generally, cannot have useful applications. PISA is a sample test that has direct impact on the time of a very small number of students, and it is not high stakes for these students. In many respects, PISA reflects the state of the art in educational measurement. Beyond mean scores and rankings, the tests generate a vast amount of information about education systems, including data relating to equity. The use of well-designed measures to "take the temperature" of education systems inexpensively and effectively is a sensible approach to testing.

However, PISA has become high stakes for some people. The assessment now acts as a report card for education ministers (Breakspear, 2014), who sing the praises of their government when performance is good or point the finger of blame when performance is poor. Politicians and media commentators are often willing to overlook the limitations of the tests, or do not have the technical expertise or time to consider these limitations, in the rush for headlines and simple political messages. People most often encounter PISA through media reports that focus on national rankings, and these are often treated as the most important outcome of PISA. Many of the crises mentioned above were prompted by rankings that did not match expectations. But there is a great deal of overpromising about what PISA can tell us and a great deal of misunderstanding about what it cannot.

This book will not offer simple solutions.

There are already enough people profiting from public education by selling simple solutions to complex problems. PISA results are often made complicit in these simplifications, including by people who are closely involved with the program. In contrast, this book aims to make educational matters more complex, but without making them more difficult to understand. We aim to help educators, parents, and others understand how PISA works in order to make critical assessments of the stories told about their schools based on PISA results. This might increase opportunities for people to engage meaningfully with what PISA *can* tell us and to join the debate about how the results *should* inform policy and practice. We aim to provide an antidote to PISA envy. But we are getting ahead of ourselves. There is an obvious question that must be answered at this point.

1.3 What is PISA?

PISA was developed by the OECD to measure reading, mathematical, and scientific literacy. PISA assesses what young people who are 15 years of age and who are enrolled in school know on a given day about content that the OECD has determined to be important for participation in the global economy. The assessment was first conducted in 2000 and has taken place every three years since then. Each cycle gives specific emphasis to one of the three domains that are assessed—reading, mathematics, and science. In PISA 2015, the major domain was scientific literacy. Later in this book, we provide an in-depth explanation of the domains and why it is important to understand the rotation of domains when interpreting and using the results.

PISA is conducted with a representative sample of 15-year-olds in each participating country or education system. The test takes two hours to complete and includes a mix of open-ended and multiple choice questions. The purpose of the test is to assess how well students can apply their knowledge and skills to solve problems based on real-life situations. PISA does not aim to test how well students have learned what is taught in schools. As well as completing the assessment, students are asked to complete a questionnaire after the test that collects further information about them, their family background, and their attitudes toward learning. School principals complete a questionnaire about their school, which enables analysis of relations between educational performance and other factors such as gender, socio-economic status, and resources. PISA also includes an optional parent questionnaire, which provides context about family, home, and learning environments.

PISA has become one of the OECD's most successful programs and has grown significantly since it began. Forty-three countries participated in PISA 2000 compared to more than 70 countries in PISA 2015. The OECD has also used PISA as a model for the development of several related programs, including PISA tests for schools, PISA for developing countries, and PISA for five-year-olds (the International Early Learning and Child Well-being Study). While we focus specifically on the main PISA in this book, much of the discussion is relevant to these other OECD education assessments.

Countries and education systems choose to participate in PISA (although they may be encouraged to do so by the OECD) and must pay to cover the costs of their participation. OECD countries can make decisions about the development and implementation of PISA as members of the PISA Governing Board, but non-OECD participants generally have less input in decision making. This gives the OECD significant influence in education beyond its membership. And this brings us to the next question.

1.4 What is the OECD?

The OECD now hosts the main event in the global education race. The OECD, or the Organisation for Economic Co-operation and Development, is an intergovernmental organization that promotes economic growth, trade expansion, and social well-being. Established in 1961, the OECD has 35 member countries, and its work covers many of the policy areas managed by governments. The United States is the dominant member and contributes the largest share of the organization's budget. Members are mainly European or Anglophone countries, with the exceptions being Chile,

Israel, Japan, Korea, Mexico, and Turkey. All OECD countries participate in PISA.

Education is a relatively recent focus in the work of the OECD, which is an economic organization that has an annual budget of more than €350 million, employs a secretariat of 2,500 staff, and produces around 250 publications per year across various policy areas. So how has an education program become so prominent in this context? The OECD's education work developed substantially during the 1990s when PISA and the Indicators of Education Systems project were developed. PISA has become a globally influential assessment on the back of the headlines that it generates and its capacity to change the way people think about education. It is important to remember that PISA was developed to assist the OECD with its economic mandate and that this rationale informed the assessment's framework and continues to guide its development.

People often talk about the OECD as an international think tank that wields influence and control over national governments. This is incorrect. Ministers, ambassadors, and other staff from member nations decide on the OECD's agenda and budget. The organization generally cannot compel member countries to comply with a policy position, although members do pressure one another in relation to particular issues. The OECD exerts influence by focusing the international conversation on topics that it deems important. PISA has been very effective at changing how people think about education and promoting particular solutions to educational problems. Why and how PISA has this kind of impact are key questions that we will explore.

1.5 Outline of this book

This book is organized into eight chapters. It is informed by academic research, but we aim to translate this research into an accessible format. The chapters take different perspectives on PISA, from analysis of its impact in the media to clear discussions of technical details and proposals for how we might engage with the data generated by testing programs.

The next chapter explores the role of the media in telling PISA stories. Most people encounter PISA in the form of headlines and media reports. These stories generally condense thousands of pages of analysis that are contained in the multivolume PISA report into a sensational headline and a simple narrative designed to attract readers. The chapter explains how these headlines become "memes" that can detach from the data and circulate as powerful stories about education that shape policy and practice.

Chapter 3 explains why focusing on PISA rankings can be a red herring. While rankings attract the most attention in reporting of the results, the OECD and many participating countries argue that rankings are not the most important findings. In some countries, PISA results are available for sub-national education systems such as cities, provinces, or states. These sub-national data provide a more complex picture than aggregated national scores and can potentially be more useful for policy-making.

Chapter 4 turns to the technical side of testing and explains how international large-scale assessments are constructed. This chapter begins to open the "black box" of testing for a general audience. Although we do not cover all technical details here, we introduce select topics such as sampling, achievement estimation, scale scores, trends, and assessment stakes. These topics are purposely selected to provide readers with a better understanding of why these assessments should always be understood as largely stable, yet fallible estimates of what 15-year-olds who are enrolled in school know.

Chapter 5 examines how the comparisons of performance between education systems can be complicated by cultural factors and students' familiarity with and preparedness for the test. Comparison is central to the rationale for conducting PISA; after all, the aim is to identify and learn from successful education systems. However, this chapter also explains that the arguments for educational reforms that PISA is used to justify may not be based on careful learning from other systems.

Chapter 6 considers the issue of validity in standardized testing. Validity is much more than a statistical property of tests and extends to questions about the justifiable use of data and the consequences of this use. We argue that governments can do more to ensure that PISA data are put to valid use, and we identify a role for teachers in speaking up about the effects of PISA results that potentially have an impact on teaching and learning in schools.

Chapter 7 shifts the focus from description of PISA and standardized testing to a discussion of the politics of educational measurement. This chapter cautions against some of the dangers of anti-testing positions and argues for improving data literacy among educators, parents, and others. Testing can be an important tool for monitoring system level outcomes from schools and highlighting inequalities. We argue for an approach that enables groups who are affected by testing and who have expertise about what is tested—the learning of young people—to contribute to the improvement of educational measurement through processes of technical democracy.

Finally, we sum up the arguments in the book with a hypothetical scenario. Imagine you have a few minutes to speak with your education minister, and she or he uses PISA results to argue that schools in your country are in crisis. As a teacher or parent with a good knowledge of schools, you disagree. But how would you respond? Would you know why your minister is caught up in an education race and whether she or he is running in the right direction? We hope this book will help you with these questions.

2

Stories

2.1 Making headlines

The success and influence of PISA is due in large part to the headlines it makes. PISA results are released every three years, and much attention is focused on comparing the performance of different countries and systems. Around the world newspapers herald the outcomes: "Top test scores from Shanghai stun educators" (*New York Times*, 7 December 2010); "UK stagnates as Shanghai tops league table" (BBC News, 3 December 2013); "Schools fail again, OECD finds" (*Australian Financial Review*, 7 December 2016); "Canadian students rank fourth for science performance" (*Globe and Mail*, 6 December 2016). PISA has become one of the OECD's most significant media events, and efforts are made to inform journalists of the results and to generate coverage across a variety of media platforms.

The headlines generated by PISA largely focus on rankings of performance in the major domain that was assessed and on whether countries are improving or declining compared to previous assessments. While the OECD explains that less than 1% of its PISA report focuses on league tables, a much higher percentage of the media reporting *does* focus on these tables. Thus, most people's only or primary contact with PISA is with rankings that reduce thousands of pages of complex analysis into a single idea: "our schools are falling behind," "we have a mathematics crisis," or "Shanghai has the best education system in the world."

As we mentioned earlier, when asked about the best education system in the world, many people point to Finland or somewhere in East Asia. When Finland ranked number one in reading literacy in PISA 2000, it was catapulted into the international spotlight, and the same thing happened when Shanghai topped the rankings in 2009. But if we look to the 2011 results of the Trends in International Mathematics and Science Study (TIMSS), another international assessment like PISA, we can see that Finland performs in the top 10 across different areas of the assessment, but not at the very top of the rankings. If we only had TIMSS, then far fewer people would know about Finnish schools. TIMSS also measures something different from PISA. It is a retrospective assessment of whether students have mastered what is taught in grades 4 and 8, whereas PISA is designed to assess students' preparedness for employment in 10 or more years' time. But because PISA attracts much greater media coverage, Finland is widely considered to be the world's top education system.

2.2 Changing the story

The official purpose of PISA is to evaluate the school systems of OECD members and other participating countries by assessing the performance of students who are enrolled in school. From an economic perspective, PISA measures human capital at the end of compulsory schooling to predict the future capacity of a nation's workforce. But this is only a partial explanation. PISA is used to make comparisons and to create conditions in which to change policy and learn from other systems. A more complete explanation of the purpose of PISA, then, is to (a) predict the future capacity of a nation's workforce to (b) change how people think about educational performance and, in turn, (c) create conducive conditions for education reform.

As the economist Milton Friedman famously observed, "Only a crisis—actual or perceived—produces real change." The OECD makes clear that programs such as PISA produce information that can generate a sense of crisis and appetite for reform:

> . . . the release of a highly publicised report on
> disappointing education outcomes or perfor-
> mance may engender a sense of crisis, not because
> educational outcomes have suddenly changed,
> but because assessments of those outcomes have.
> (OECD, 2010, p.355)

PISA produces *catalyst data*. A catalyst is something that encourages a process of change. The act of simply producing PISA data can provoke change regardless of what the data say about performance. If the results are good, then action must be taken to sustain this level of performance, and people will want to visit and learn from the successful system. If the results are average or poor, then something must be done to improve. PISA results can change the way people think about education simply by producing information about outcomes that was not available previously. What matters most here is not a change in *outcomes*, but rather a change in *measurement* of those outcomes.

Consider the example of Germany's performance in PISA 2000. Before the results were released in 2001, many in Germany believed their schooling system was a world leader, even though in earlier international assessments they had not performed well. But when Germany was ranked 22nd for reading literacy by PISA, a national debate was sparked about the quality of German schools. What changed at this point was not the *ability* of German students as readers, but the *information* upon which judgments of their reading ability was based. In other words, PISA moved the goalposts to tell a new story. This reminds us that any story about an educational crisis told using PISA relies on a more or less explicit assumption that PISA produces the right information for reaching this conclusion. If this is not true, then PISA may well be of less concern to those who make education policy.

2.3 Getting the word out

Government ministers who are responsible for education are the primary audience for the analysis and advice provided by the OECD. Of course, this poses the challenge of how to attract attention from politicians to an international data set that may seem distant from the more immediate concerns of their constituents. There is also a significant financial imperative to meet this challenge, because governments that take PISA seriously are more likely to continue supporting and funding the program. The OECD devotes considerable effort to generating high profile media publicity as a way to capture the attention of politicians and the people who vote for them. If PISA generates headlines that decry a country's falling performance or failing schools, this places pressure on politicians to respond and strengthens the influence and perceived importance of the assessment.

Leading up to the release of PISA results, which usually occurs in December of the year after it is conducted, the OECD shares the findings with journalists and helps them understand the details. The organizations that have responsibility for administering PISA in each country also contribute to this work by issuing media statements and producing country-specific reports. Journalists are provided with embargoed materials before the public announcement of results. This provides time for them to craft their stories. Of course, journalists are also driven by the imperative to capture the attention of as many viewers or readers as possible, and this can encourage them to sensationalize their stories. The PISA results are publicly launched at events in cities such as Paris, Washington, London, and Brussels. Time is spent giving interviews to as many journalists as possible and providing an overview of the findings to various audiences.

Social media also play an important role in communicating the PISA results. The OECD media unit and the director of education and skills at the OECD actively promote the release of PISA on Twitter. Lobby groups, such as StudentsFirst in the United States, have also been very active on Twitter following the release. The StudentsFirst website is structured according to a straightforward "crisis and solution" narrative, and PISA results are used to support this story. Another example is the Alliance for Excellent Education, which hosts a PISA Day website to promote the findings. Some of the most influential non-government actors in US education support the alliance, including the Bill and Melinda Gates Foundation and the William and Flora Hewlett Foundation. In Canada, Facebook groups and blog posts have been used to promote stories of crisis in relation to declining PISA mathematics performance. The OECD sits at the centre of these mainstream and social media networks that amplify the stories that get told about PISA.

There are two important points to emphasize here. First, while the OECD actively promotes PISA to the media, many other groups also draw attention to PISA and use the results to create narratives about the need for change that align with their particular agendas. Second, after the initial media splash created by the release of PISA, some stories persist, or can even gain momentum, as memes that become detached from their basis in the PISA findings. In other words, PISA stories can take on a life of their own.

2.4 PISA memes

A meme is an idea that repeats and spreads from person to person. The concept can be traced back to the work of the evolutionary biologist Richard Dawkins, and it is useful for understanding PISA stories because the simplification of findings as headlines can produce ideas about education that spread and evolve over time. The information captured in PISA memes can gradually change thinking about education in significant ways. The media and those who have vested interests in shaping educational debate are often active in such PISA contagion.

MEMES

One obvious example of a PISA meme is the idea that Finland has the world's best education system (Sahlberg, 2015). When Finland ranked top in reading performance in PISA 2000, it drew international attention to Finnish schools and gave rise to a small industry in edu-tourism. People from all over the world visited Finnish schools to learn about their education system and schooling practices. Much academic attention was directed to analyzing and theorizing why Finland performed so well and to drawing lessons for other education systems. This commentary and analysis helped solidify the idea that Finland is a world leader in education, and the idea has spread far beyond those who know about PISA. Indeed, we have now reached a point where people tend to project their own views of "good education" onto Finland (Waldow, Takayama & Sung, 2014). In some cases, ideas about "good Finnish education" have become detached from their basis in PISA data and have taken on a life of their own, with effects on educational policy-making and educational debate globally.

Research organizations and think tanks have also contributed to the creation of PISA memes by holding meetings

and publishing reports that canvass reform directions based
on PISA data. For example, following PISA 2009, the National
Centre on Education and the Economy in the United States
published a report titled *Surpassing Shanghai: An Agenda
for American Education Built on the World's Leading Systems*.
In Australia, the Grattan Institute published a report titled
Catching Up: Learning from the Best School Systems in East Asia.
Both reports emerged from high-level meetings between
politicians and bureaucrats in which staff from the OECD
participated. Both reports translate the stories that the United
States and Australia are falling behind East Asian education
systems into a set of catchy ideas that are designed to spread
among policy-makers. In other cases, think tanks may incorporate PISA data into their own reports and rankings, amplify-
ing some messages while overlooking others. For example,
The Conference Board of Canada publishes a K–12 education
report card that compares provincial performance using PISA
data. Reports of this kind extend the influence of PISA beyond
the assessment and into subsequent debates about educational reform and economic competitiveness. PISA memes can
have many hosts.

Finally, while the results of PISA are released every three
years, the OECD aims to keep PISA in the news by releasing
monthly notes that provide analyses of PISA data in an accessible format for journalists and policy-makers. These notes—
PISA in Focus—analyze one aspect of the PISA data to address
a specific question, such as "Who are the low-performing
students?" The OECD employs this strategy to repeat and

evolve PISA stories during the periods between assessments
to maintain interest and keep the program topical.

2.5 Conclusion

Telling and retelling PISA stories is not simply a matter of
creating fictions. These stories may initially have a firm basis
in the data generated by the assessment, and it is natural for
people to seek out the most important messages from a very
large and diverse report. Few people have time to read the
thousands of pages of reporting about PISA that the OECD
produces, and the realities of the media dictate that simplifications are necessary. But these stories reduce the complexity of the PISA findings to simple messages that are aimed at
changing or reinforcing particular perceptions of education
and influencing the decisions of policy-makers. It is important to keep in mind that stories produced by PISA necessarily leave out the important details required to make informed
assessments of whether a particular meme should spread or
whether some skeptical medicine is required.

Consider this example. Following PISA 2012, a story cir-
culated in Alberta, Canada, about a mathematics crisis in the
province's schools. The story was based on PISA results that
showed Alberta's mean score in mathematics had declined
substantially since 2003. The story was used by some to make
a case for "back-to-basics" reform of the mathematics curriculum. We can say that the story about decline is true, but
it is not possible to infer that this was caused by a specific
problem with the Albertan curriculum. Understanding that

PISA is not designed to measure how well students learn the curriculum taught in schools, and that many systems with different mathematics curricula also experienced declines in mathematics performance from 2003 to 2012, would create less fertile conditions for this meme to spread.

The power of PISA is substantially attributable to the stories that are told about the results. A large proportion of these stories focus on comparisons between countries based on rankings of mean scores. The first step in deciding which stories to believe and which to dismiss is to understand some of the issues with the rankings. This is the task of the next chapter, and it will clear the way for a more nuanced understanding of the data PISA generates.

3

Rankings

3.1 Policy by numbers

What goes into a number? When it comes to PISA, it turns out to be quite a bit. For example, the PISA 2012 report spans six volumes and runs to nearly 2,500 pages. There are numerous supplementary analyses and technical reports detailing the work that went into designing and conducting the assessment. The raw data are also made publicly available, but the data files come with a warning that some users may have trouble downloading them due to their large size. PISA generates an extensive database that is subject to careful and diverse explorations by the OECD and researchers from around the world.

All of the statistical work that underpins PISA enables the production of a few numbers that capture most of the attention. When country representatives to the PISA Governing Board were asked about what aspect of the results led to change in policy or practice in their countries, the rankings and reading performance scores were the two elements that were considered to have the clearest impact (Breakspear, 2012). This is unsurprising given that busy policy-makers who do not have time to wade through complicated and often ambivalent details look for readily digestible "take home" messages.

But this is a problem. Countries are best grouped as high, average, and low performing, rather than as occupying specific individual ranks. There is always a degree of error in assessments and small differences that lead to the ranking of one country ahead of another may not be significant enough to say, conclusively, that the two countries performed differently. In such cases, focusing on small differences in the rankings may divert attention from what the data actually tell us. The aim of this chapter is to delve further into this issue and to discuss why a focus on rankings or average scores can divert attention from more interesting and useful aspects of the PISA data.

3.2 More than a ranking

An open letter published in the *Guardian* on 28 April 2014 criticized PISA for the emphasis on rankings and comparisons in the reporting of results. The director of education and skills at the OECD responded that "less than 1% of the PISA reporting is devoted to league tables," as we mentioned earlier. Of course, this is less than 1% of the official OECD reports and *not* less than 1% of the media coverage, but the important point is that PISA findings are much broader than rankings of national performance in reading, mathematics, or science.

Rankings may not be the information of most interest to participants. Many countries that receive low rankings are not surprised. In fact, when low-performing countries participate in the same PISA assessment as OECD countries, the assessment does a very poor job at evaluating what students know or how different populations within the country perform. The OECD has introduced a new program, PISA for Development, to provide better information for developing countries. There is ample evidence that countries participate in PISA for a much more varied array of reasons than simply determining where they are placed in the global education race. For some, participation is a way to join a global community in conversation about education. For others, participation may be a strategy for developing technical capacities in educational assessment.

Many OECD staff maintain that rankings are not the most useful aspect of PISA. Indeed, this message is now emphasized when releasing the results. The OECD's media relations strategy aims to provide journalists with a more nuanced narrative about a country's performance than is captured in a single score or a comparison against other participants. However, there is pragmatic recognition within the OECD that the media will want league tables, and the OECD does promote narratives about the decline or improvement of scores in a given country and its performance in comparison to other nations (Baroutsis & Lingard, 2016). While the official OECD position is that rankings are not perfect, and are not the most important aspect of the results, the OECD has built the PISA brand on the attention that these numbers attract.

3.3 Who is really ahead?

In its technical documentation, the OECD explains that it is not possible to assign an exact ranking to countries based on their average scores in reading, mathematics, and science. As such, in some reporting, the OECD carefully backs away from ranking countries and instead separates them into three groups: those which are significantly (in statistical terms) above the OECD average; those which are not significantly different from the OECD average; and those which are significantly below the OECD average. This may come as a surprise given the attention directed to the rankings and the anxiety produced among policy-makers when their countries slip below others. However, it is important to note that when the OECD does report scores, countries are ordered by achievement, and error estimates are not consistently reported. In other words, exact rankings are not exact. Rankings are not really accurate unless the size of the errors associated with the rank are presented.

An informed discussion of performance comparisons between different countries requires looking beyond the rankings to see whether a difference in rank position reflects a statistically significant difference in average performance between countries. For example, in PISA 2012 it is only possible to be confident that Shanghai, China, ranked number one and Singapore ranked in second place; all other countries had achievement estimates that were not significantly different from at least two other participants. Our confidence regarding Shanghai's position as the number one ranked participant points to another issue. PISA enables the ranking and

RANKINGS

Rankings can hide a lot of technical work and uncertainty. We should not assume that a country that is ranked 3rd for reading has performed more poorly than the 2nd ranked country and more highly than the 4th ranked country. And if the same country falls to 6th place in the next round of PISA, we should not assume this indicates a significant decline in performance.

Consider these two examples:

1. The Netherlands was ranked 10th with a score of 523 for mathematics in PISA 2012. However, this score was not significantly different from 9th placed Switzerland's score of 531 or from the scores of Estonia (which placed 12th), Finland (13th), Canada (14th), and Vietnam (17th). We can say that the Netherlands placed somewhere between 9th and 14th, but we cannot be certain that they had the 10th highest score.

2. Denmark scored 497 for reading in PISA 2000 and was ranked 17th. In PISA 2009, it scored 495 and was ranked 24th. A focus on the rankings would produce the alarming story that Denmark had dropped seven places, but taking a closer look at the scores suggests that reading performance was not significantly different in Denmark in 2003 and 2009.

comparison of different entities: national education systems and sub-national education systems such as Shanghai. While Shanghai's strong performance has drawn attention to education in China and East Asia more broadly, we should be careful when comparing apples and oranges. In PISA 2015, when Shanghai was combined with other Chinese sub-national education systems, science performance was not significantly different from that in the United Kingdom, Slovenia, or Australia, among others.

3.4 Running in multiple places at once

Countries that participate in PISA usually do so on the condition that the results are included in the official reporting. An important part of the OECD's ethos is the commitment of member nations, and others participating in OECD programs, to contribute to a collective project of generating data for policy. However, in the case of China, the OECD has assessed many regions but only published the full results for Shanghai in 2009 and 2012, and an average score for the combined regions of Beijing, Shanghai, Jiangsu, and Guangdong in 2015. Allowing a country such as China to choose to release results on its own terms demonstrates the political stakes of PISA and the importance to the OECD of including major economies, even if this means bending the rules.

As Chan and Seddon (2014) show, the PISA 2009 results were available for 12 Chinese regions. Shanghai was the strongest performing region with a score of 556 for reading. Zhejiang placed 2nd of these regions with a score of 525, which is comparable to nations that ranked around positions five and six overall. The lowest-ranked Chinese region had a score of 407, which is comparable to countries that placed around 60th in the rankings (bearing in mind the caveat that scores are best seen as ranges, not specific numbers). Indeed, if China's performance was compared based on the average score for all 12 regions in 2009, rather than Shanghai alone, it would have received a score of 486, which is below the OECD average and comparable to countries that ranked around the 30th position. We can see here that Shanghai's performance is not representative of performance across China more generally.

China is not the only nation in which results can be disaggregated for sub-national units. Other countries, such as Canada and Australia, draw a large sample of students from across their provincial or state education systems to enable comparisons between them. This oversampling enables us to look beyond national averages to a more fine-grained analysis of performance in different systems and among different student groups. In Canada, for example, there is a great deal of variation in performance across the provinces. (Note: only British Columbia, Alberta, Manitoba, Ontario, Quebec, New Brunswick, and Nova Scotia had representative samples.) National averages hide important differences between these sub-national school systems.

Based on 2012 results, we should be wary of claims that mathematics is in decline in Canada *as a whole*, given that Quebec and Saskatchewan have not shown significant decline. Moreover, the focus on decline in Alberta, as mentioned earlier, can push aside important details. Alberta was not the only province to show decline. In fact, eight other

TABLE 1. RESULTS IN PAPER-BASED MATHEMATICS—CANADA AND PROVINCES

| | 2003 | | 2012 | |
	AVERAGE	SE*	AVERAGE	SE WITH LINKING ERROR**
CANADA	532	1.8	**518**	2.7
NEWFOUNDLAND AND LABRADOR	517	2.5	**490**	4.2
PRINCE EDWARD ISLAND	500	2	**479**	3.2
NOVA SCOTIA	515	2.2	**497**	4.5
NEW BRUNSWICK	512	1.8	**502**	3.2
QUEBEC	537	4.7	536	3.9
ONTARIO	530	3.6	**514**	4.5
MANITOBA	528	3.1	**492**	3.5
SASKATCHEWAN	516	3.9	506	3.6
ALBERTA	549	4.3	**517**	5.0
BRITISH COLUMBIA	538	2.4	**522**	4.8

Note: Results in bold indicate a statistically significant difference compared with the baseline (2003).
* SE = Standard error.
** The standard error of measurement includes a linking error to account for the comparison of results over time between the baseline (2003) and subsequent years.

Canadian provinces also showed declines, and so did 13 other participating countries. While there is alignment between curricula in certain Canadian provinces, it is important to note that the decline in Canadian performance does not seem to correspond with curriculum priorities in particular provinces, as is sometimes claimed.

3.5 Interpreting the results

While an aggregated score is important for national policy-making, a decline in the national average may occur at the same time that a sub-national system shows improved performance. Such complexities become particularly important when one hopes to draw policy lessons from PISA. Telling national stories about PISA performance in systems where sub-national data are available may produce red herrings that mislead those looking for evidence to inform policy.

The example of Australia is instructive here. A narrative of decline has characterized discussion about PISA in Australia over recent years and has permeated the public debate about Australian schools more generally. Declining PISA performance has become a meme and it is common to hear people speak about Australia falling behind without any mention of PISA and without unpacking the nature of this decline. One response has been to set a target to improve Australia's position in the PISA rankings by 2025, based on the national average score. This response signals that addressing PISA performance has become a challenge for the nation and an end in itself.

However, as Gorur and Wu (2014) have shown, some education systems in Australia performed much better than the national average score of 515 for reading in PISA 2009. Indeed, the Australian Capital Territory (ACT) scored 531, which would place it around 5th in the overall rankings and is not statistically different from Hong Kong (2nd) and Singapore (3rd). In contrast, students in the Northern Territory performed similarly to those in nations that ranked in the mid-30s. It makes little sense to draw the conclusion, as some have done, that Australian school systems should be looking toward East Asian education systems for policy lessons based on Australia's national average score and ranking. Moreover, even at the national level, it may be more appropriate to look inward than outward. In Canada, Prince Edward Island has historically scored lower than most provinces and may learn a great deal more from British Columbia than systems outside Canada.

RESPONDING TO THE RANKINGS

Consider how two different systems responded to the PISA 2015 rankings. We chose Norway and the Canadian province of Alberta to contrast different responses from highly developed economies. Both systems are resource-rich economies with a similar population of around five million. Given the structure of the Canadian educational system, provinces are largely independent from the national government and thus can be easily compared to other national systems.

Norway has a checkered past when it comes to PISA. Several authors have discussed how the test has influenced the educational system and the reforms that have followed from poor PISA results (Norwegian Directorate for Education and Training, 2011). Yet, when discussing the PISA 2015 results, Norwegian Minister of Education Torbjørn Røe Isaksen stated that "there are many indications that we are on the right path. We must thank the teachers and principals for the important work they do" (The Local, 2016, para. 6). These largely celebrated results in Norway consisted of no statistical difference in score change over three years in science (498) and math (502) and a modest 5 point increase in the minor domain of reading (513). The positive tone of the Norwegian minister's initial remarks shows how average and largely stagnant scores can be seen as progress.

Unlike Norway, however, Alberta has historically been a strong performer on PISA. Similar to its neighbour, British Columbia, Alberta was an early star in PISA 2000 and largely maintained this status. In fact, PISA 2015 performance in science (541) and reading (533) showed that Alberta was a world leader in both subjects (outperforming PISA darlings such as Finland). However, in math, Alberta scored slightly lower than 2012 (511), yet still well above the OECD average of 490. On the day the 2015 results were released, the minister of education, David Eggen, used the less-than-perfect PISA results as a call for promoting his administration's plan to improve math performance in the province (CBC News, 2016). Unlike in Norway, the initial response of the government was focused on what needed to be improved rather than what was accomplished.

These two short examples are not intended to summarize comprehensive responses by governments to PISA 2015. In contrast, they are intended to demonstrate that two governments can initially react to PISA results in completely different ways. As such, it is important to recognize that PISA is often not about the results but rather about the narrative leaders want to promote. Norway wanted to show that its results were either stable or improved and thus that its system was improving. On the other hand, in Alberta, constant improvement was the narrative with little room to celebrate the past administration's accomplishments.

3.6 Conclusion

The rankings generated by PISA capture much of the attention while also hiding much of what is potentially useful about the findings. A change in ranking does not necessarily mean that there has been a significant change in a country's performance, and when one country ranks a few places below another country, it does not necessarily mean that we can be confident that the performance of the two countries is significantly different. Clearly, Shanghai's top ranking in reading in PISA 2009, 17 points ahead of second-ranked South Korea, tells us that something was happening in Shanghai. But in many cases, the rankings are a poor place to turn for evidence about performance and ideas for policy.

Countries like Canada and Australia, which have a federal system in which sub-national education systems follow different policies and implement different curricula, provide a salutary example of why focusing on national rankings can be a distraction. In these countries, we may see common patterns across sub-national systems, which would suggest that the causes of these patterns are not different sub-national policies or practices, unless they are closely aligned. We may also see variation between systems, which would suggest that sub-national policies and practices, or the demographics in different states and provinces, are contributing to these differences.

In many cases, the potential usefulness of the PISA findings depends on looking beyond national average scores and rankings to unpack the results in more detail. Where school systems are going and whether they are making progress in the right directions matters more than who appears to be in the lead at each bend. In the next chapter, we turn to a more technical discussion that provides tools for understanding the PISA tests and how they are conducted.

4

Tests

4.1 Introduction

Successfully implementing PISA requires years of cooperation from several actors, including high level policy-makers,
test developers—which can include both non-profit and for-
profit companies—content experts, school leaders, teachers,
and individual examinees. In an effort to ensure the highest
possible quality, all procedures and materials are subject to
extensive validation by panels of experts. However, in spite
of the care with which PISA is developed, any study of such
scope and ambition will necessarily have limitations.

In what follows, we attempt to provide an overview of
some key technical details about PISA that are important for
all assessment consumers to understand. Of course, given
the inherent complexity of testing over 70 educational systems, there are numerous issues that could be covered. For

interested readers, the PISA Technical Report provides a wealth of information on how the test is constructed. But at nearly 500 pages, the technical report can be an overwhelming place to start. As such, we have selected topics that we feel are important to understand for all who are interested in international large-scale assessments. With even a basic grasp of the issues outlined below, one can begin to appreciate why these assessments should always be understood as a fallible estimate of what 15-year-olds who are enrolled in school know on a given day about the content that the OECD has determined to be important for full participation in the global economy.

4.2 Sampling participants

Consider the resources that would be necessary for testing all 15-year-olds in the United States and Canada. With populations that number in the millions, the time and money required would be enormous. Fortunately, we know from sampling theory that a much smaller but representative sample from a population of interest can provide highly accurate results at a fraction of the cost. To that end, PISA employs robust sampling methods that require only a few thousand students and a two-hour block of testing time per student. With a carefully developed protocol that is produced in accordance with strict technical standards (OECD, 2014), this approach allows us to draw inferences from a much smaller sample to the larger overall population of 15-year-olds in schools. But although PISA's sampling methods are well-established, sampling nevertheless introduces some error into the overall score.

To select students for participation, PISA generally uses a two-stage stratified sample design. This simply means that PISA first selects a sample of schools from the participating system (at least 150) and then in the majority of countries a random sample of forty-two 15-year-olds, regardless of grade, is chosen in each school. This sampling process results in a minimum of 4,500 students being drawn in each system. In Canada, a larger sample was selected to produce reliable estimates for each province. As such, in Canada approximately 20,000 15-year-olds from about 725 schools participated in PISA 2015 across the 10 provinces. PISA samples are intended to be representative of the target population (15-year-olds in school), but not necessarily 15-year-olds in general.

In spite of the care with which samples are drawn, the sampling process will necessarily suffer from deficiencies. For example, in some participating systems, more schools are excluded from the sample than the normally accepted threshold of 5%. In other participating systems, there are large populations of 15-year-olds who are not enrolled in school, and it is thus difficult to say that the tested 15-year-olds truly represent the population. For a more detailed discussion of sampling in PISA, see OECD (2014) and Rutkowski and Rutkowski (2016).

As samples are drawn to represent some population, users of PISA data should be aware of these sampling issues because they can call into question what is being compared. For example, it could be the case that 98% of 15-year-olds are included in the sample in country X and only 60% in country Y. In PISA 2012, 16 participating educational systems (including top-performing Shanghai) captured less than 80%

of all 15-year-olds in their country (OECD, 2014, p.268). At the extreme, Costa Rica covered just 50% of all 15-year-olds, while Albania and Vietnam covered 55% and 56%, respectively. This suggests that nearly half of the population of all 15-year-olds were not included in the sampling frame. And although this is not an inherent sampling problem (as indicated by a well-covered target population), it certainly makes comparison difficult because some countries are including most of their 15-year-olds and other countries are not.

A related issue is that PISA draws a sample from the population of 15-year-olds attending educational institutions in Grade 7 and higher (OECD, 2012, p.62). Of course, the amount of schooling someone receives can play an important role in what students know and can do. The choice of an age-based sample (15-year-olds) versus a grade-based sample (8th grade students) is an important factor in how we talk about PISA in relation to schools. Assessing 15-year-olds who participated in 7 to 12 years of schooling rather than students who have had the same years of schooling (e.g., sampling 8th grade students regardless of age) can be problematic. Given that some schooling systems have had more opportunity to instruct students compared to others, it is difficult to connect the schools' influence on learning in many participating systems. In other words, one student in Canada may have had 7 years of schooling and another 10 years; but in Norway, most participating students have had 9 years of schooling. If you want to know what the two groups were able to learn from 15 years of life experience, comparing an age-based sample is appropriate, but if you want to know what Norwegian and Canadian students were able to learn from school, the comparison is fraught with issues.

4.3 Achievement estimation (national scores)

To attain stable estimates of achievement in all domains, PISA would normally require the administration of over 10 hours of testing time. Such a burden is unreasonable in most situations, and so assessment experts employ a sophisticated design to estimate achievement. This design means that each student takes a portion of the entire assessment. In other words, just as PISA samples participants, PISA also samples assessment items (albeit the processes are not entirely the same).

Using what is called multiple-matrix sampling, test material is divided up into overlapping item clusters that are assembled into partially overlapping test booklets so that approximately 10 hours of testable material is packaged into 120-minute booklets, one of which is administered to each student sitting the test. The technical details are complex, yet well-established (OECD, 2014). At the individual level, this process results in each student receiving five possible scores, called plausible values, for each subject that is tested. Remember, an individual student does not take the entire test, but only a part of the assessment, and the testing organizations use their background information along with how students performed on a portion of the test to calculate five likely scores. When we aggregate this process to the population level, the scores are stable; however, at the individual and school level, the testing organization simply does not have enough information to calculate accurate scores. As such, these five scores should never be reported as individual results. In addition, given the above estimation process, results from PISA should not be reported at the school level.

All reported PISA results should include a statistical measure of uncertainty, which quantifies multiple error sources in the results. This measure of uncertainty, or standard error, is normally reported in brackets directly following the PISA score. For example, the PISA 2015 science achievement of Alberta 15-year-olds was estimated as 541 (4.0) and 15-year-olds in British Columbia received 539 (4.3). This suggests that the OECD is 95% confident that Alberta's score was between 537 and 545, while British Columbia was between 534.7 and 545.6. Because there is overlap in the estimated scores, we are not able to conclude that the scores differ between Alberta and British Columbia. This is one reason why rankings are best understood as ranges rather than exact places. In addition, we contend that reporting standard errors is more than simply good statistical practice. Standard errors remind all stakeholders that PISA scores are not exact, but rather estimations of what the OECD believes 15-year-olds know and can do.

STUDENT BACKGROUND QUESTIONNAIRES

PISA includes several questionnaires that are administered to a range of stakeholders. In 2015 these included the school questionnaire distributed to school principals; the student questionnaire distributed to all participating students; two optional questionnaires for students: the educational career questionnaire and the Information and Communication Technology (ICT) familiarity questionnaire; an optional questionnaire for parents; and an optional questionnaire for teachers. Here we would like to focus on the student questionnaire as it is important to creating and contextualizing achievement scores.

The students' 35-minute background questionnaire is administered after the student completes the two-hour portion of the assessment. The student questionnaire seeks information about the students themselves, their homes, and their school and learning experiences. The core context of the student questionnaire includes questions focused on three areas: student and school background; processes; and non-cognitive outcomes. Table 2 provides some information on the types of questions that are asked. Interested readers are encouraged to consult the PISA framework (OECD, 2016a), where they can find examples of all questionnaires that are administered by PISA.

TABLE 2. STUDENT LEVEL MEASURES INCLUDED IN CORE STUDENT BACKGROUND QUESTIONNAIRES

	STUDENT AND SCHOOL BACKGROUND	PROCESSES	NON-COGNITIVE OUTCOMES
FOCUS OF STUDENT LEVEL QUESTIONS	Gender, socio-economic status (parents' education and occupation, home possessions, number of books at home), language and migration background, grade level, pre-primary education, age at school entry	Grade repetition, program attended, learning time at school (mandatory lessons and additional instruction), out-of-school learning	Domain-general non-cognitive outcomes (e.g., achievement motivation, well-being in school) Domain-specific non-cognitive outcomes (motivation, domain-related beliefs and strategies, self-related beliefs, domain-related behaviour)

Source: (OECD, 2016a)

There are clear limitations with how background questionnaires are currently administered. First, given the limited
time, the questionnaires cannot include all aspects important
to understanding educational achievement. Second, the
cross-cultural challenges of administering one questionnaire
to a diverse set of countries should not be underestimated.
Cultural differences in concepts such as confidence and
academic self-concept most certainly exist. Even a concept as
universally important as socio-economic status is challenging
to define and measure across a variety of educational systems
(Rutkowski & Rutkowski, 2013). As such, the OECD must find
an agreeable compromise and only include those questions
that are relevant to the majority of systems. Finally, student
motivation and focus may not be optimal after completing
a two-hour low-stakes assessment. To date, how these and
other factors influence the results of PISA and subsequent
analysis is not well understood.

4.4 Scale scores and assessment type

In PISA 2000, test developers provided a scale with an average score of 500 for OECD countries and a standard deviation
of 100 for each assessed subject. The choice of 500 is arbi-
trary and developers could have chosen any scale (e.g., an
average score of 1,000 or 80,000). The standard deviation of
100 means that in PISA 2000, approximately 68% of OECD
students had an estimated score between 400 and 600, 95%
between 300 and 700 and 99.7% between 200 and 800. After

the PISA 2000 cycle, the international average for reading (major domain) was no longer fixed at a mean of 500, partly so that stakeholders could observe change over time. During the next cycle of PISA in 2003, mathematics was the major domain and the OECD average was set to 500 with a standard deviation of 100. The average was allowed to adjust freely after that cycle. The same process occurred for science in 2006. Importantly, the OECD average is now allowed to change from cycle to cycle in all domains. For example, in the most recent round of PISA 2015, the OECD averages fell from the original set score of 500: reading to 493; mathematics to 490; and science to 493.

Allowing the scores to adjust over time can add confusion regarding whether PISA is a criterion- or norm-referenced test. Criterion-referenced assessments are those where achievement is compared to a standard or learning objective and not the performance of other students. As such, all students who take the assessment can theoretically reach the highest achievement standard. In addition, with criterion-referenced tests, measurement over time or between populations is possible. Norm-referenced assessments compare an individual to a larger group (i.e., the norm). In the case of PISA 2000, the larger group or "norm group" was the international sample of OECD countries. What this means is that PISA scores were norm referenced in 2000, but now can fluctuate depending on how well students perform on the criteria set by the OECD. The fact that the OECD averages have remained close to the "normed" average of 500 set in 2000 is a result of the extremely large sample undertaken in each cycle of PISA. While it may be a bit of an overstatement to call PISA a criterion-referenced test, it is equally problematic to call current versions of PISA norm-referenced.

4.5 Trends

Since 2000, PISA has assessed student performance in three core domains: mathematics, reading, and science. Testing three subjects is an ambitious task. Nevertheless, PISA added the domains of problem solving in 2003 and 2012, financial literacy in 2012 and 2015, and complex problem solving in 2015. Each PISA cycle emphasizes one core domain, termed the major domain, leaving the other two core domains as minor (see Table 3).

TABLE 3. MAJOR* AND MINOR DOMAINS ASSESSED

			ASSESSMENT YEAR			
	2000	**2003**	**2006**	**2009**	**2012**	**2015**
SUBJECT ASSESSED	**Reading**	Reading	Reading	**Reading**	Reading	Reading
	Math	**Math**	Math	Math	**Math**	Math
	Science	Science	**Science**	Science	Science	**Science**

Note: The subject in bold is the major domain for the given year.

In 2009, the major domain of reading was allocated 60% of the testing time, whereas the other 40% was evenly split between mathematics and science (OECD, 2012, p.28). Given that the majority of testing time was allocated to reading, PISA 2009 more thoroughly assessed reading when compared to mathematics and science. Further, the additional time allocated to reading allowed for the inclusion of more "linking items." Linking items allow test developers to ensure that the assessment is comparable from cycle to cycle and that changes in scores are due to student performance and not differences in the assessment between cycles.

More linking items lessen the link error in score comparison between cycles. In PISA, the link error is statistically accounted for and documented in the PISA technical reports (e.g., OECD, 2012). Link error estimates provide information about how trends were estimated in PISA. They are also useful for independent researchers who are interested in understanding trends in PISA. Along with sampling errors, link errors manifest themselves in the measures of uncertainty that surround achievement estimates across time.

Also relevant to the major/minor domain distinction is the fact that the frameworks for PISA were not well-developed until the point at which they served as the major domain: 2000 for reading, 2003 for mathematics, and 2006 for science. Consequently, mathematics achievement is comparable only back to 2003, and science achievement is directly comparable across cycles only back to 2006 (OECD, 2012). In addition, given the small number of overlapping linking items between major and minor, or minor and minor domain years (e.g., reading in 2000 and 2003) it is only advisable to compare performance differences between major domains (e.g., reading in 2000 and 2009). In other words, because the minor domains only include a small number of questions, we do not have enough linking items that are similar between the previous test and the current test to be confident that the changes in scores are due to changes in student ability.

4.6 Stakes

Understanding the stakes of PISA can be complex. In their most general form, high-stakes assessments have proximal consequences attached to results; for example, assessments used to determine grades, promotion, college admission, or a scholarship. On the other side of the spectrum, low-stakes assessments have less proximal consequences but can, and often do, have some consequences in an indirect way. As such, when we talk about stakes, it is important first to consider the group with whom you wish to associate the stakes. For example, PISA may be a low-stakes assessment for students, but it can be high stakes for policy-makers. In addition, even though PISA may be a low-stakes assessment for students, it can and often does have significant consequences for educational systems and can certainly influence students' educational experiences. For this reason, it is important that a wider audience understand how PISA may be shaping education in their schools.

4.7 Conclusion

Reviewing the technical documentation from 2000 to 2012 illustrates that PISA has historically been innovative as well as carefully developed and administered. Yet any project of this size and scope will suffer from technical issues that will inherently influence the results. As a way to underscore the importance of interpreting and using PISA results with caution, in this chapter we discussed select interrelated methodological issues. Our intention is not to explain the details of these issues, but rather to describe select areas that should help those who wish to use results of international assessments to understand school systems.

Even under the very best circumstances, PISA is, by definition, an assessment in select content areas (intentionally divorced from curriculum) that is administered on a single day to a sample of 15-year-olds that are enrolled in school. In an ideal setting, the PISA design and sample limits inferences to a narrowly defined population regarding their performance on a narrowly defined set of topics. Based on rigorous technical standards, the information provided by PISA is acceptably precise and reliable; however, it is not perfect. And any interpretation of PISA results should be made in light of the test's limitations, not in ignorance or obfuscation of them. We certainly acknowledge that PISA's methodological limitations are known, recognized by the methodological community, and not limited to PISA. Unfortunately, as demonstrated in previous chapters, there is a growing amount of evidence that these limitations are not being clearly and simply communicated to the broader scientific, policy, and practice communities. More care needs to be taken to ensure that the results are understood as fallible measures.

In the following chapters, we will move beyond these technical issues to discuss broader questions of comparison and the validity of making claims based on PISA. Technical issues discussed in this chapter are important in that they limit what PISA can tell us about our educational systems. However, as will be noted, even if we develop better ways to sample, estimate achievement, or measure trends, we are still left with

the very real questions of what we can compare using PISA
and how PISA should be used to make valid inferences about
educational performance.

5

Comparisons

5.1 Comparison gets complicated

Comparison is something we do constantly as we navigate
our daily lives. We compare prices at the supermarket, the
different routes we could take to and from work, or our ath-
letic ability when we compete in sporting events. Comparison
has also become a powerful tool for governing people, organizations, and systems. PISA generates a raft of indicators
that are used to compare different aspects of education, and
these comparisons inform public debate and policy-making.
International assessments such as PISA enable comparisons
between performance at different times within a single system, like national testing, but also comparisons between different systems at a single point in time.

Some comparisons are unproblematic. For example, comparing the weight or dimensions of two different objects is
straightforward. But comparison becomes more complicated

when we try to measure complex things, particularly cultural things such as "literacy." One kilogram is one kilogram in Japan and the United States (or at least it can be easily converted as 2.20462 pounds), but literacy is not necessarily the same thing in both places. Comparing literacy across different education systems requires, first, a shared belief that literacy can and should be measured and compared, and then consensus regarding what will be counted as literacy. Much work is required to produce tools that will reliably measure the same thing in different places.

The question of who decides what "counts" is important when measuring and making comparisons. What counts in PISA is decided by a range of different groups, including the PISA Governing Board and the technical agencies that help construct the tests. In this chapter, we consider (a) how the testing situation can affect what a test item measures, with implications for what gets compared; (b) how culture appears to be associated with PISA performance, which raises a question regarding whether PISA compares the quality of education systems; and (c) how comparisons between performance get used for policy-making.

5.2 What are we comparing?

PISA is designed to measure how well students can apply their knowledge and skills in "real-world" situations (see Figure 1). However, there is a strong argument that the primary real-world situation in which PISA tests the ability to apply knowledge and skills is the testing situation itself (Dohn, 2007). In other words, we can argue that PISA tests how well young

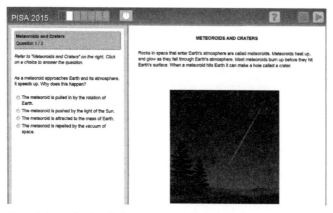

Figure 1: A sample scientific literacy test item from PISA 2015.

people can complete tests such as PISA. People who are familiar with testing of this kind may be in a better position to perform well on the tests than people who are less familiar with these situations (see The Mongolian Camel, p. 58). Moreover, many students now take the tests on a computer rather than using pencil and paper. Some demographic groups (e.g., boys) can be advantaged by this mode of test-taking and this can affect the results (Jerrim, 2016).

Another little-discussed factor in relation to PISA is the different level of preparation students receive for the assessment. In Australia, students who are identified by the sampling process are taken out of class for two hours to sit the test. In many cases, students have little understanding about what PISA is or why they are taking the test. In contrast, Scottish students sitting for PISA 2012 were prepared for the test. These students were shown a short motivational video that compared their efforts to those of Scottish athletes and encouraged them to do their best to represent their country. In Mexico, a more extensive and systematic campaign was established to prepare students, including a website, radio announcements, and manuals for teachers and students that familiarized them with the test and provided opportunities for practice. Clearly, students who have been told that a test is

---

THE MONGOLIAN CAMEL

Consider the example of the Mongolian camel. While this case relates to UNESCO's Literacy Assessment Monitoring Programme (LAMP) rather than PISA, it provides a good research-based illustration that performance on assessment items can be affected by familiarity with taking tests. Maddox (2014) showed that people in Mongolia were strongly engaged in one of the LAMP test items that focused on Mongolian camels. Given that people in Mongolia are generally familiar with these camels, they were expected to perform well on this item. However, Mongolian test takers proved no more likely to answer this item correctly than other test takers. The Mongolian test takers had *too much* context and answered the question based on their real-world expertise (i.e., their knowledge about Mongolian camels) rather than a critical reading of the text that framed the test item (i.e., providing the specific information requested by the test). Test takers in other countries who knew relatively little about camels, but who were more familiar with reading test items and seeking out the required information, performed just as well. In this case, what is being compared is not necessarily knowledge about camels, but knowledge about tests.

---

important and have been prepared for the test will approach it differently than those who do not understand what they are doing or why they have been asked to do it.

The translation of test items is another issue that must be kept in mind. PISA items are initially written in English and French and are then translated into 90 other languages used in the countries and systems that participate. The translation verification process is extensive; however, in some cases, the translation of test items can make them more or less difficult to answer correctly. For example, a test item may be translated correctly from a technical point of view, but the structure of the target language may increase the difficulty of the item. While the OECD takes care to remove items that function differently in different places to reduce the effect that context, culture, and translation might have on what is being measured, the difficulties of ensuring the same thing is being measured in different languages and contexts cannot always be easily overcome (Berliner, 2015). Fortunately, to date there has been no conclusive evidence that translation issues have a meaningful impact on the methods used to estimate PISA scores.

5.3 The importance of culture

The OECD promotes PISA as a measure of how well education systems prepare students for work and life, and policy-makers are encouraged to learn from successful or improving systems. However, there are good reasons to suspect that PISA also measures the effects of culture on educational performance. For example, Feniger and Lefstein (2014; see also Jerrim, 2015) have shown that students in Australia and New Zealand who come from a Chinese cultural background perform comparably with students in Shanghai, China. The Australian and New Zealand students included in this analysis had only attended schools in Australia and New Zealand, but performed better than their non-Chinese peers. If students who have only participated in Australian schools perform as well as Chinese students in Shanghai schools, as this analysis suggests, then is it reasonable to conclude that Shanghai schools are better than those in Australia? The simple answer is that we cannot be sure that PISA measures the relation between the quality of education systems and student performance in reading, math, and science.

School factors have also been shown to have a relatively minor impact on performance on standardized achievement tests. School factors account for around 20% of variation in scores in standardized assessments (Haertel, 2013). In contrast, out-of-school factors such as cultural background or socio-economic status account for around 60% of variance. So it makes sense that students with similar cultural backgrounds could perform similarly, even when they have been schooled in different systems, taught by teachers trained differently, and have learned different curricula according to different pedagogical approaches. For example, Chinese students in Australia and Shanghai may both receive high levels of encouragement from their families to do well at school. Equally, students with different cultural backgrounds and social contexts who are schooled in the same system may also perform very differently because out-of-school factors affect their learning in school. Indeed, PISA shows us that students from low socio-economic backgrounds perform more poorly than their peers from high socio-economic backgrounds.

The fact that Chinese students in different systems perform similarly does not necessarily undermine the comparisons between education systems that can be made using PISA data; again, it just means that we need to dig deeper than comparisons of system level scores (e.g., Shanghai compared to Australia). By breaking down performance by cultural groups, we can learn that different groups in the same system perform differently and can then ask questions about why this might be. Or by breaking down performance on individual items, we can learn about strengths and weaknesses in a particular system. As Gorur and Wu (2014) have shown, an item-by-item analysis of mathematics performance in PISA 2009 shows that top-ranking Shanghai, China, performed relatively poorly on some items, and Australia, which ranked 15th overall, was a top performer on other items. It may be more useful to focus attention on particular areas where a sample of students have performed poorly, rather than lamenting mathematical performance across the board and making sweeping changes that could be counterproductive in areas where students are already performing well.

5.4 Learning from others

One of the primary rationales for conducting PISA and using the data it generates to compare different education systems is to identify strong performing systems and to learn from these systems. As we have explained, Finland's top performance spawned a phenomenon of edu-tourism as policy-makers and educators visited Finnish schools to discover what makes them so successful, and Shanghai's strong performance since 2009 has had a similar effect. The OECD, in conjunction with the philanthropic foundation of the education company Pearson, have also produced videos that provide snapshots of the policy settings that ostensibly contribute to strong performance or successful reforms in a select group of countries, and the PISA reports contain numerous examples of policy and practice that might be borrowed by policy-makers and educators looking for evidence-based policy ideas. However, the policy learning enabled by PISA is complicated by cultural and contextual factors that may affect performance and, in many cases, reforms spurred by PISA do not involve substantive learning from other systems.

The example of Chinese students who performed well on PISA in Shanghai, Australia, and New Zealand suggests that systemic policy may be less important than culture when understanding the performance of these students. If performance can be attributed, at least in part, to cultural background and family context, then this raises the question of whether it is reasonable to look to Shanghai schools for policy ideas that can be borrowed to improve Australian school systems. Put simply, education policy is not necessarily the main contributor to PISA performance, and thus it is important to tread carefully when looking elsewhere for lessons on how to improve.

Another issue is the use of league tables and comparisons to scandalize or glorify performance and to justify the need for reform (Steiner-Khamsi, 2003). References to the performance of other education systems may be used to drive a particular policy agenda. The high performance of other systems may be used to argue for the need to improve by groups who are seeking education reform. In this case, PISA data are not used to *learn* from other systems, but rather to support pre-existing arguments for educational change.

In other cases, the success of a particular country may not be considered worthy of emulation if its success is perceived as being purchased at too high a price. For example, South Korea performs well in PISA, but the pressure placed on young people to succeed at school and the time spent studying outside of regular school hours are seen by many as a high cost to pay for this success. There are high levels of anxiety and unhappiness among South Korean students, which are measured by the PISA background questionnaire (although we must exercise caution when interpreting single-item rankings). Indeed, Korea is the bottom-ranked nation in terms of the percentage of students who report being happy at school (Figure 2). While South Korea performs very well, policy-makers in other countries have been less inclined to search for policy lessons in South Korean schools because this system is perceived as a negative example, rather than a model to be followed.

The relation between ideas borrowed from other systems and the realities in those systems can be quite tenuous. Waldow, Takayama, and Sung (2014) explain that looking elsewhere for ideas can sometimes involve "policy projection," in which the features of the external system that appear most salient are those that are most relevant to internal debates. For example, Waldow (2017) has described a case in which, following Germany's PISA shock in 2001, a German

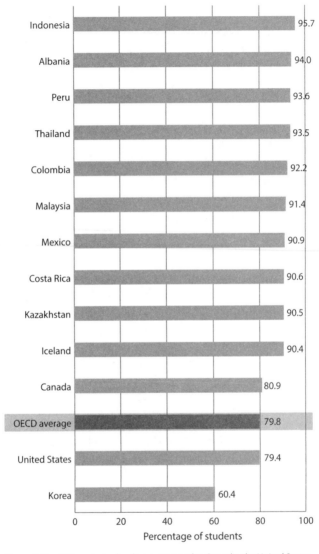

Figure 2. Top 10 happiest schooling systems, plus Canada, the United States, and Korea

newspaper reported that one reason for Finland's top performance was all-day schooling, which was a point of debate within Germany at the time. However, Finland did not have all-day schooling, and the mistaken emphasis on this aspect of the Finnish system said more about the state of educational politics in Germany than it did about actual Finnish education structures. In this case, PISA was a catalyst for educational change, but the reforms that were proposed were not developed from evidence-based policy learning.

Even though comparison is promoted as a basis for directing attention to successful policies in high-performing systems and learning about "what works" in education, the relation between external reference systems and internal education reforms can be complicated. Remember, a key function of PISA is to open windows for policy reform, but this does not guarantee that such reforms will draw on research evidence rather than being driven by a particular political agenda.

5.5 Conclusion

A lurking issue throughout the discussion in this chapter has been the question of causality. Much of the public debate about PISA implies that particular factors contribute to high performance ("Teacher mentoring contributes to strong performance in Shanghai" "Teachers with Master's degrees contribute to strong performance in Finland"). However, we must be clear about what "contribute" means here. Can we say that certain factors are a cause of PISA performance, or only that they are related to performance? Answering this question becomes important if we follow the PISA rationale of

measuring and comparing educational performance across
countries to identify what works.

An elementary point that is made in any introduction
to statistics is that correlation does not imply causation.
Although two variables may be correlated, we cannot say that
that one causes the other. A quick Google search will return
a range of humorous correlations that show how problematic it is to make the leap from correlation to causation. For
example, total revenue generated by computer game arcades
in the United States correlates with the number of computer
science doctorates awarded, but this does not mean that play-
ing more Donkey Kong will improve one's academic ability.

One approach to international comparisons in education
that has been popular is to connect a measure of education
with Gross National Product (GNP). This gives rise to claims
that changes in what is measured cause increases in GNP. PISA
data have been used for this purpose to argue that increasing
PISA performance will yield increases in GNP. This is problematic. First, there are the issues with measuring education
outcomes that we have raised. Then there is the challenge of
theorizing the relationship between education and a complex
construct like GNP to specify a model that controls for all the
relevant variables. We need to be sure that decline in performance is caused by teachers not undertaking Master's level
study, for example, rather than students spending too much
time at the arcade when they should be studying.

There is a long-held view among economists of education that accurately measuring the relation between education and productivity is impossible (Klees, 2016). We should
be wary of any claim that changes in test performance will

cause related changes in national economies, or that a particular variable can be isolated from the complex array of factors that affect schooling systems to specify that it causes improved test performance. Indeed, the director of education and skills at the OECD frequently cautions against such misunderstandings in relation to PISA data. The fact is that PISA is a cross-sectional assessment that happens every three years and not an experimental study purposely designed to show causal relations. Further, although some researchers argue that statistical techniques can overcome the inherent design issues of PISA and mimic causal results, the validity of doing so has yet to be established.

PISA does produce data that can enable useful comparisons, but the problems arise when stories are told about PISA that over-attribute causality and become detached from their basis in the data. Comparison is central to the rationale for PISA of identifying and learning from successful education systems. However, much care must be taken with the inferences that we make using PISA data, and in the next chapter we turn to this question of validity.

6

Validity

6.1 Introduction

One of the key questions for all large-scale assessments is how
the data should be used. Often there is a belief that tests some-
how speak for themselves and test data can simply and clearly
point policy-makers in a particular direction. However, this is
not the case, and an ongoing problem with PISA is that participant countries[1] often do not recognize *their* responsibility to set the agenda for PISA, to specify clearly its uses and
limitations, and to define the goals of PISA in national contexts. The assumption that improved performance is enough
is highly problematic. To increase the usefulness of PISA, educational jurisdictions should create meaningful procedures

---

1 We use the phrase "participant countries" as an inclusive term to indicate
all school systems that participate in PISA, regardless of whether these are
national or sub-national systems or whether they are OECD members or
non-members.

and protocols that improve the educative benefit of PISA, rather than perpetuating the focus on rankings. An engagement with validity theory can help with this task.

While much criticism has been levelled at the OECD for problems with test design and the assumed commensurability of what PISA measures, there has been much less attention given to what countries do with the data. Due to its design, PISA does not provide results that teachers can directly use in their classrooms. However, the OECD is reaching out more directly to teachers through resources such as *Ten Questions for Mathematics Teachers . . . and How PISA Can Help Answer Them* (OECD, 2016b). While it is too early to judge how effective these resources will be in the long term, PISA has become high stakes for governments, and these stakes invariably become policy drivers that have an impact on schools, teachers, and students. If this is the case, then we should include teachers in debates about how PISA data are used and the validity of these uses.

The numbers produced through testing (such as individual scores, average scores, and comparative rankings) do not themselves constitute meaning. Rather, the meaning given to test scores (at its most basic level, the notions of a "good" or "bad" score) requires a leap from the numbers to judgment about what these scores signify and what should be done. This leap from the psychometric to the inferential is complex and is one focus of validity theory. In this chapter, we briefly sketch one view of validity and suggest an approach through which participant countries could engage thoughtfully and meaningfully in evaluation of how PISA data are used in their context.

6.2 Validity is more than the properties of the tests

PISA—like all standardized tests that use samples of the population drawn from a relatively small number of schools—accesses a relatively limited, yet important, subset of knowledge that is used to generate a variety of inferences. The relevance and usefulness of PISA data depends on the inferences that can be *validly* drawn. Among the many challenges that PISA presents to us, the question of how we can make valid inferences from the data is particularly important.

There are many approaches to validity, but there is also general consensus that validity is one of the most important considerations in educational assessment. We define validity "as the extent to which the proposed interpretations and uses of test scores are justified," which requires "conceptual analysis of the coherence and completeness of the claims and empirical analyses of the inferences and assumptions inherent in the claims" (Kane, 2016, p.198). Validity is a pragmatic undertaking that involves demonstrating that tests are sound and considering how tests are used to inform policy and practice. For PISA, this requires participant countries to conduct empirical evaluations of how test scores are used to generate meaning. Such processes of evaluation are central to making better use of the tests, but are generally not done well, if at all. Issues of quality control also mean that such evaluations should not be the responsibility of the OECD.

The American Educational Research Association, the American Psychological Association, and the National Council for Measurement in Education have published the *Standards for Educational and Psychological Testing*, which focuses on defining validity for large-scale standardized assessments. The *Standards* is regularly revised to incorporate new information, techniques, and approaches. While this report contains extensive technical insight and detail, there are some critical points that bear on PISA:

- Test use is as much a matter of validity as (statistical) score interpretation.
- Each use (inference) of the test needs to be validated.
- All tests need to be clear about how the scores are statistically validated and how the uses of the data are being evaluated for their validity.

Adhering to these principles can create problems. While test developers and psychometricians might know about the intended uses of test data, they often have very little first-hand experience of how these data actually get used in schools and systems. We cannot think of a group that has better experience of how tests scores are used in schools than teachers and principals. Thus, the voice of teachers is important in understanding which, if any, inferences from test data affect their work. While the OECD includes teacher and teacher union reference groups in the design of PISA, we also see a role for educators in the validation of PISA by contributing to understanding what the results say about their specific context and what should be done.

6.3 Validity theory

Many models of validity have been developed over the past 100 years. Since the 1980s, test designers and assessment experts have struggled with reconciling the statistical (or broadly speaking, scientific) aspects of test design and evaluation with the consequential (or ethical) realities of testing. Accurate test data on its own cannot improve school systems; it is how it is interpreted and used that is crucial.

Validity is an evaluative judgment of the degree to which empirical evidence and theoretical rationales support the *adequacy* and *appropriateness* of *inferences* and *actions* based on test scores. As such, validity is an inductive summary of both the existing evidence for, and the potential consequences of, test interpretation and use. What is to be validated is not the test as such, but the inferences derived from test scores—inferences about score meaning or interpretation and about the implications for action that these interpretations entail (Messick, 1987, p.1). Using data in more valid ways, which are attentive to the limits of the statistical analysis and the dangers of simple correlations, does have the potential to provide useful information for educational systems.

Most teachers receive little training in assessment literacy. Teacher education, with few exceptions, does not help teachers understand data, evidence, and validity, despite this being perhaps the most crucial understanding when using assessment data. This is important for two reasons: (1) some uses of test data can pervert the intent of the tests by altering the constructs for which the tests are designed and calibrated, and (2) the promiscuous use of test data can imply that test scores can be put to uses beyond those for which they have been validated.

We propose that valid use of test scores could be improved by adopting an *argumentative approach*, where each intended use of the tests scores must be argued for and subsequently evaluated. Proposing that each use, or inference, of a test needs to be argued for draws on Michael Kane's argumentative approach to validity. Kane suggests that for validity to be workable, it should be broken into two distinct parts: (1) the *interpretative use argument* (IUA) and (2) the *validity evaluation*.

The IUA is the sequence or network of inferences that stretch from test scores to the conclusions or inferences drawn from test performances. As Kane (2013, p.11) argues, the mode of an IUA is generally one of presumptive reasoning, extending along an "if . . . then . . . " line of argumentation. For example: "**If** a student gets X questions correct on the test, **then** we suggest that the student has attained level Y in construct A." This is an interpretative argument in which the inference is made about the relationship between the observed performance and the observed score. If a student gets 20 out of 20 on a standardized test of reading comprehension, then we can infer that the student is performing at an excellent level in reading comprehension. Of course, tests like PISA are less concerned with individual student performance than with what individual performances, when aggregated, can tell us about (a) the sample who sat the test (the generalization inference) and (b) the wider population and the conditions in which this population is considered to be operating (the extrapolation inference). The journey from an interpretive inference to an extrapolation or theoretical inference is a move from simple numerical representations (i.e., a score of 20 out of 20) to arguments about what this score means and how this meaning could be extended to make other, broader, judgments.

The IUA encompasses the statistical generation of scores, the analysis, the presentation of that analysis, and its relation to what is measured. We should stress that the OECD conducts detailed statistical analysis of the tests as evidenced in their technical reports. The PISA 2012 Technical Report (OECD, 2014) shows that validity is defined in its scientific forms in relation to issues as diverse as cross-cultural comparativeness (p.51), forms of statistical analysis (p.53), school sampling (p.80), data management and tracking (p.171), and construct validation (p.314). The OECD takes the scientific validation of PISA very seriously, but, understandably, we cannot find evidence in the technical reports of evaluations of how PISA data are being extrapolated in educational systems.

HOW NOT TO PISA

In PISA 2000, Australia scored near the top of the table. This result was largely confirmed in PISA 2003. While many celebrated the success of Australia's schools, several researchers were left scratching their heads. The Australian education system had several structural challenges, including problems with equitable outcomes for Indigenous students, more and more middle-class students leaving public education to enroll in private education, a federal system where states developed their own curriculum and assessment strategies, and ongoing logistical problems with providing schooling to rural and remote communities. Australia was successful according to the rankings, but no one was really sure what led to this success. From PISA 2006, when results declined, successive Australian governments implemented polices designed to nationalize education and to hold teachers to account for student performance. These reforms included introducing a national testing regime with results posted on a public website to promote parental "choice," the introduction of a national curriculum, and the creation of the Australian Institute for Teaching and School Leadership, with the mission to develop and maintain rigorous Australian professional standards for teaching and school leadership, to control teacher accreditation, and to regulate university teacher education.

In 2013, the Australian government passed the Education Act 2013. This legislation enshrined in law that the goal of the Australian education system was to be "Top 5 by 2025" in PISA. This is an astounding move. Rather than PISA serving to evaluate the policies and processes that have been implemented to deliver quality and equitable education, PISA has become the goal of education policy. The PISA 2015 results show that the decline in Australian students' scores has continued. Commentary from politicians on this decline indicates that Australia still has little understanding about why it was successful in 2000 and 2003, what has caused the decline, and what should be done to reverse this trend, except to intensify the accountability and regulatory regimes already in place. The aim of reversing the trend of declining PISA scores seems to be to improve PISA scores through intensifying those policies that have not worked so far. A bold move.

Of course, there is an obvious reason for the OECD's narrow focus on the validity of the tests, rather than the consequences: this is the domain for which the OECD has responsibility. While there is a commonly held view that the OECD acts in its own interests, the ambitions and interests of its members actually constitute its agenda. These members and other participant countries must assume responsibility for evaluating the use and consequences of the tests in each specific context. With this in mind, we have several suggestions for participant countries regarding their responsibilities for validity.

Kane's argumentative approach requires that all IUAs be evaluated, as a whole or in part, and subject to empirical scrutiny to try to falsify interpretations. As Cronbach (1980, p.103) suggests: "The job of validation is not to support an interpretation, but to find out what might be wrong with it. A proposition deserves some degree of trust only when it has survived serious attempts to falsify it." For example, one current inference is that PISA measures the quality of an education system. This claim must be evaluated within each system in which it is made. Arguing for the use of test data to infer that test scores can be used as indicators of teacher quality, for example, or whether the ranking of national systems based on PISA data is meaningful, requires both test developers and test users to present satisfactory evidence that these are reasonable inferences. As Kane (2013) argues:

> To make a positive case for the proposed interpretations and uses of scores, the validity argument needs to provide backing for all of the inferences in

> *the IUA and to rule out any plausible challenges
> to the IUA. It is important to specify the IUA in
> enough detail so that the weakest parts of the IUA
> can be identified and evaluated. (p.1)*

International large-scale assessments such as PISA are rarely subject to an examination of plausible challenge, particularly by the governments that pay to conduct the tests.

6.4 Evaluating validity

We propose that participant countries should clearly define what inferences will be made from PISA results and how the evidence we currently have supports the use of tests in these ways. Participants should take a long-term view, remembering that students who sit the tests began their education around 10 years earlier. Participants should accept that evaluating the validity of the inferences made from PISA data is their responsibility. This requires ongoing evaluation. If we think of participation in PISA in terms of opportunity costs, particularly given the way that it takes oxygen from other education debates, it seems strange that participant countries assume little responsibility for what is done with the results. Moreover, a significant part of this evaluation could involve teachers and principals, who can provide important insights on the inferences being drawn from PISA in relation to classrooms and schools.

In light of these proposals, we want to return to the problem of comparison discussed earlier. Across the period of its existence, PISA has suffered from several criticisms concerning how the progression is made from tests to claims about quality, equity, and comparability. Here we consider, as examples for discussion, two questions about validity derived from research that has identified problems with making the leap from scores to meaning without considered evaluation.

> *Example 1:* Is it valid to compare comprehensive school systems with selective school systems, particularly in those systems where significant numbers of students (usually under-performers) cannot access education services and, as such, cannot sit the tests? For example, Loveless (2014) calls into question the population of 15-year-olds that were included in the sampling frame for the top-performing system Shanghai. He argues that children of rural Chinse citizens who move to the city and tend to be less educated are not allowed in Shanghai's official schools. Loveless argues that excluding this group may have significantly improved Shanghai's performance. In other systems, such as Vietnam, only a little more than half of the country's 15-year-olds are enrolled in school. Is it valid to compare samples from these populations to a system that includes most 15-year-olds in their sampling frame?

> *Example 2:* South Korea has always ranked highly on PISA. However, South Korea is well-known for the prevalence of its private tutoring industry, or what Bray (2009) calls the "shadow education" industry. In 2011, it was estimated that 72% of South Korean students accessed private tutoring, and this cost South Korean families $18 billion USD a year, which is equivalent to 80% of government expenditure on primary and secondary education (Korean National Statistics

Office, 2012; cited in Choi, 2012). Choi (2012) suggests
that prohibiting private tutoring in South Korea
would decrease average test scores by 0.47 standard
deviations. If the same effect were observed on PISA,
this would suggest that, without private tutoring, South
Korea would perform at an average level of educational
achievement. The point is not whether South Korea
should or should not have private tutoring, or the
extent of that tutoring. Rather, the question is whether
it is valid to infer that PISA results in South Korea and,
for example, Alberta, Canada, reflect differences in
schooling rather than external systemic and cultural
factors. This is important because participant countries
should be clear about the educational policies and
structures they are willing to pursue in the race for
higher rankings.

6.5 Conclusion

One of the big challenges when using PISA data is the ease
with which correlations become causal claims in general discussion about the results. For example, there is a tendency
to look for single causes that can be associated with results
and targeted by policy solutions. A classic example is when
a decline in performance is assumed to result from a single
factor, such as a change in curriculum, even though curriculum changes usually take a long time to have an impact
on outcomes. This is not to suggest that these factors do not
contribute to performance, but rather that wider social and
structural factors also affect performance in complex ways.

Taking an argumentative approach to validity is one strategy for addressing elisions between correlation and causation when making claims based on PISA data.

To conclude, we propose that teachers and principals should be encouraged to ask the following questions of their systems and system leaders when PISA data are assumed to provide evidence for a particular issue.

1. What additional evidence has been gathered to support the argument that is being made using test results?

2. What attempts have been made to evaluate whether or not this interpretation is reasonable?

3. What are the plausible challenges to this inference that have been ruled out? If no plausible challenges have been identified and ruled out, how can you be confident that the argument is justifiable?

4. What is my government or jurisdiction doing to improve both the understanding and use of PISA in my context? Who is setting the agenda regarding what PISA can, and should, be used for? Who is conducting ongoing evaluations to ensure that the limitations of the tests are recognized so that the best possible use can be made of the results?

7

Politics

7.1 Rethinking testing

In October 2015, President Obama announced a new approach
to standardized testing in the United States that would reduce
the number of tests students are required to take. In a country that has been at the forefront of the standardized testing
movement, this shift served as a bellwether of changing sen-
timent globally. In Australia, England, and Canada in recent
years there have been several anti-testing movements driven
by parents, educators, academics, and teacher associations.
Perhaps the most well-known and powerful of these has
been the opt-out movement in New York State. This chapter
moves our discussion from a description of how PISA works
to a consideration of the politics of educational measurement. How should parents, educators, and others who are
concerned about standardized testing respond to programs
like PISA?

We have attended many events in which people have spoken against standardized testing and accountability regimes that sanction and reward teacher and school performance as measured by tests. However, it is not uncommon to see PISA data used at such events to support a case against testing or to promote a case for more equitable education systems. For example, we have seen data from PISA used to argue that countries with high levels of standardized testing also have relatively high numbers of students with low literacy. In this case, the argument was made that testing is not improving literacy—you cannot fatten a pig by measuring it—and thus high levels of testing cannot be justified. We have also seen PISA data used to show that education systems where resources are more equitably distributed show higher levels of performance (indeed, one of us has used PISA data in this way), while at the same time arguing against test-driven modes of educational accountability. In both cases, testing data is used to support a critique of over-testing or the misuse of testing data.

We think this is how it should be. While there will certainly be cases where there is too much testing or where particular testing regimes cannot be justified, we do not endorse a general anti-testing position. Instead, we argue for informed, critical engagement with testing that aims to (1) help improve the quality of data generated about education systems and (2) support the use of data in valid ways that may improve educational outcomes for all students. In some cases, this may mean abolishing a particular testing program if it does not do what it promises or if it has negative or perverse effects. We believe it is possible to reject a particular test without rejecting the possibility that educational measurement can be a useful tool when used judiciously for valid purposes.

Opposition to testing builds its platform on shaky ground when it begins from the position that education simply cannot be measured or that educational testing is inherently antithetical to learning. These positions reject testing and the data it generates based on universal assertions about the nature of education (e.g., "For all people at all times it will not be possible to measure what matters most about their education"). This claim precludes the possibility that we might learn more about education or develop new and better tools for measuring it. Moreover, these positions often juxtapose testing data with evidence drawn from idiosyncratic accounts of students' experiences in schools (e.g., "What is most important for my child is X"). Evidence of this kind is not useful for policymakers who are responsible for making difficult decisions about how to fairly meet the needs of all children in large and diverse school systems. In our view, such anti-testing positions face serious challenges, and in this chapter, we begin to sketch an alternative critical politics of educational measurement.

7.2 Testing and climate change

In recent years, some scholars working in university humanities and social science departments have been relatively successful at challenging the authority of modern science. While science is commonly understood as a process of discovering facts about reality, and at the same time discrediting false beliefs, these scholars have argued that facts are *made* not *found*. From this point of view, science is understood to be a process of social construction whereby the rules followed by scientists enable them to show that a particular claim cannot be proven false and is thus a fact. This view can weaken the authority of science because it suggests that facts tell us more about the rules of scientists than they do about reality.

The social constructivist argument has been important in showing how science operates in the real world and in encouraging critical attitudes toward science. However, people holding these positions can find themselves with strange bedfellows. Consider the example of climate change. There is now a substantial body of scientific evidence indicating that humans are contributing to the warming of the globe. Indeed, the future of the human species may well rest on convincing enough people that these claims are facts that demand attention and action. However, there are also large numbers of people who reject this evidence and deny that the climate is warming. Those who deny the evidence do not feel beholden to the same rules as scientists and thus feel free to reject scientific claims. Their power to reject science comes from the same source as that of its social constructivist critics: rejection of science's authority to demand our acknowledgement of the facts it produces. We now live in "post-truth" times.

The question that we want to raise here is whether rejecting evidence generated by educational testing, on the basis that education cannot be measured, is similar to the rejection of climate change on the basis that evidence about human contributions to global warming cannot be measured. Is this a fair comparison to make? And if so, should anti-testing positions reconsider their role in discrediting measurement as a tool for rational understanding?

7.3 Fair measures

One reason for rejecting the above comparison would be that educational measurement is not science. For a hypothesis to become a scientific fact, it must undergo a long and complex process in which specific methods are used and particular processes are followed before a scientific finding is announced as a new discovery. PISA does not involve any experiments and there are no hypotheses that get tested. But PISA can share something important with scientific research if it does not play fast and loose with causal claims and follows a rigorous and transparent methodology. And there is a very good reason for respecting transparent and standardized measurement as a tool for understanding social systems: fairness.

Standard measures enable things to be compared and exchanged fairly. If you pay for one litre of milk, then you can expect the container of milk you receive to have a volume of one litre. If you receive less than one litre, then an injustice has occurred, and you are entitled to demand restitution for the gap between what you paid for and what you received. Educational measurement also shows us when there are gaps between what people expect to receive from schools and what they actually receive. For example, when a testing program shows that students in the same school system perform very differently, this can create an imperative for change to improve the outcomes of low-performing students. It is for this reason that some civil rights groups in the United States have been critical of movements that have resisted testing by opting-out. One glaring difference between this example and testing, however, is that we are much better at measuring the volume of milk than knowledge. There is room for improvement with regard to the latter.

Good measurement is crucial for ensuring fairness. We see this principle upheld every time someone uses measurements from PISA to make arguments against intensifying standardized testing or for equal distribution of resources to ensure fairer outcomes from schooling. However, if you use PISA data in this way, then you cannot simply dismiss other of the program's findings unless you can make a strong argument as to why the measurements that support your positions are correct while others can be dismissed. This is like accepting scientific claims when they underpin the antibiotics you need to treat an infection, but rejecting scientific evidence when it supports inconvenient truths that do not fit with your business interests.

We see a need for increased data literacy and consistent approaches to evidence in education, not politicized opposition to educational measurement. Just as climate science deniers should not be able to dismiss evidence that has implications for all of humanity on the basis that it does not fit with their beliefs, anti-testing activists should not dismiss educational measurement according to the belief that it is and always will be impossible to measure the important outcomes of education. However, we do endorse the position that those concerned with education should have a platform on which to challenge tests that are of dubious quality, tests

that are being misused, or over-testing that risks distorting
the educational experience, and attainment, of children for
reasons such as corporate gain.

7.4 Improving educational measurement

Of course, we recognize that measuring education is difficult
and contentious. We admit that there are great challenges in
the way of being able to confidently claim that what is defined
and measured as literacy in the United States, Brazil, and
Vietnam is the same thing. But PISA is perhaps one of the
best efforts that has been made to accurately measure educational outcomes, and it does provide education ministers,
education activists, educators, and parents with data about
equity that can be used to argue for changes that could make
education systems fairer and better. However, these data
draw on measures of performance, and it is not possible to
have one's cake and eat it too. If we want data on who wins
and who loses in our education systems, then we need system-level measures of how well students are performing. To
this end, we are interested in approaches that enable educators, parents, and others to discuss, contest, and potentially
help improve educational measurement.

Coupling standardized testing with punitive regimes of
educational accountability is one sure way to generate negative and perverse effects. Political lobby groups and governments have created a view that teachers cannot be trusted,
and thus "hard data" are needed to make sure that they are
doing their jobs properly. The positive potential of educational measurement is eroded when data are gathered and

used by one group of people to make potentially high-stakes judgments and decisions about another group of people. Jeffrey Henig (2013) has written that:

> *Wariness toward the corrupting potential of interest group politics has led us to harness data tightly within administratively designed incentive systems; in the process, are we missing opportunities to inject data more forcefully into the public sphere, encouraging democratic accountability by parents and citizens who become, over time, more confident and knowledgeable about how to use data to collectively define priorities and select educational strategies? (p.xii)*

When standardized testing is used as a tool for governments to manage and control teacher performance, it can quickly run into problems. But are we missing other opportunities for educators, parents, and citizens to debate and decide what "counts" in their schools and to help shape how it is counted?

7.5 Technical democracy

In 2007, the town of Pickering in Northern England was badly damaged by flooding (Whatmore & Landstrom, 2011). Many in the community had been calling for the Environment Agency to defend the town from flood events, but the process had stalled when a proposed flood defence wall failed a cost-benefit analysis and was resisted by some in the local community on aesthetic grounds. Hydraulic modelling showed that a wall was the only feasible option, but some opponents could not understand why dredging the waterway would not fix the problem. Anyone who has dealt with a blocked drain could see the appeal of the latter solution. The situation reached an impasse.

In this context, a group of academics, led by Professor Sarah Whatmore from the University of Oxford, began a project that brought together experts in hydraulic modelling and people from the local community. The Ryedale Flood Research Group provided a forum in which experts could teach community members about their models and community members could test their theories about how to solve the problem. Eventually, the combination of scientific expertise and local knowledge about water catchments in the region led to a novel and effective solution: creating small dams in strategic locations to slow the passage of water into the town during heavy rain events.

Could we imagine creating similar groups to address the controversies of testing in schools? In situations where educational measurement is contested as tool for addressing educational problems, could groups be established "in which the direction given to research and the modes of application of its results are discussed, uncertainties predominate, and everyone contributes information and knowledge that enrich the discussion" (Callon, Lascoumes & Barthe, 2009, p.9)? This is the possibility that has animated the writing of this book. We see possibilities for improving data literacy among educators, parents, and others to enable forms of technical democracy in which complex matters such as educational measurement are neither rejected out-of-hand or simply left to the experts. Rather, we would like to see a wider and more informed debate about standardized testing and, in particular, the role that PISA should and should not play in national education policy-making and in shaping the work of teachers in classrooms. This is one way we can begin to tell new and different stories about PISA.

7.6 Conclusion

It is time for a new approach to the politics of educational measurement. We understand the concerns of educators and parents who reject particular standardized testing programs, and we respect political movements that have been successful in resisting testing in situations where it does not benefit students, where it undermines the teaching profession, and where it feathers the nests of big business. Moreover, we recognize that educational measurement is a challenging project. However, we do not see good evidence for abandoning efforts to develop and improve our measurement tools in education, particularly when they provide system-level information that policy-makers need to make decisions aimed at ensuring all young people get the outcomes they deserve from their schooling.

We do recognize the importance of ensuring that PISA does not have perverse or negative effects on policies and practices in school systems. For example, the purposes of education can become narrowed when PISA becomes a beacon for national education reforms, and subjects that are not assessed by PISA, such as arts and music, can suffer. Moreover, reforms that focus on improving PISA performance as an end in itself miss the point of this policy tool. PISA can have damaging effects and these should be resisted. However, circumspect use of PISA data can be beneficial, and there is an imperative to generate the best possible data and to put it to valid and effective use.

Top-down approaches to testing and educational account-ability often keep teachers, parents, and students in the dark when it comes to what gets measured and how judgments are made about performance. We see possibilities for bring-ing together experts in educational measurement and oth-ers who have different kinds of expertise—knowledge about particular students, schools, communities, pedagogies, cur-ricula, changing employment needs, and so on—to improve how we measure education and to contribute to the use of data to define educational priorities. However, this form of technical democracy, which people have been experimenting with in other fields for some time, requires informed com-munities who can see how a particular issue affects them and are willing to contribute to solutions. Our aim in this book has been to improve understanding about the technical and political aspects of PISA to contribute to the emergence of communities who could develop new approaches to educa-tional measurement and accountability in education.

CONCLUSION

Helping policy-makers
find the right track

In December 2016, the OECD released the results from
PISA 2015. The impact of these data are yet to be felt beyond
the initial headlines and the overarching message that science education is falling behind the growing pace of scientific
and technological development globally (OECD, 2016c). The
aim of this book has been to provide you with an introduction to PISA, to show how it works in technical and political
terms, and to argue for broader and more informed debate
about the use of PISA results in policy-making. We hope that
it will enable you, at the very least, to be able to talk about the
stories generated by PISA 2015 with others and to unpack
some of the issues.

The writing of this book has been animated by a belief
that people who are not expert in education assessment, but

who are concerned with education, can have something to say about PISA. Rather than arguing against testing on grounds that it is damagingly reductive or that it is impossible to quantify some aspects of learning, we have instead argued that considered use of data generated by sophisticated testing instruments has a role to play in education policy-making. In a world being dramatically reshaped by data, we consider improving data literacy among people concerned with education to be a crucial project. In the coming years, data-driven technologies will become increasingly prevalent and powerful in education, and the future of "public" education will depend on the creation of publics who understand enough about these technologies to debate their benefits, dangers, and impacts on the collective project of teaching the next generation.

With this shared task in mind, we will conclude with a short hypothetical situation. Imagine that you find yourself in an elevator with the minister for education in your country, state, or province. There have been several damaging reports in the media about how poorly schools are performing, and people have been talking about the need for curriculum change and more teacher accountability. The minister fears falling behind in the global education race and is scrambling to catch up. Having read this book, you think the situation is complex, and you want to explain why education is not necessarily in crisis and why a race to reform can lead in the wrong direction if you don't have the right information. Here we provide you with seven points to help you have this conversation.

Point 1: Stories told about PISA are not always what PISA tells us.

PISA was developed to support evidence-based policy-making. The headlines that PISA generates condense large volumes of data and analysis into simplistic messages that can create a sense of crisis and the view that education reform is required. These stories can become memes that are disconnected from the data that spawned them, and it is the responsibility of governments to ensure that reforms driven by PISA are based on evidence, not myth.

Point 2: PISA can only tell us about what it measures.

The OECD is an economic organization that aims to promote the prosperity of its members and a global free market economy. The OECD designed PISA to help achieve this goal. At best, the data produced by PISA represent what the OECD has decided 15-year-old students should know in the subjects of mathematics, reading, and science. Your system may have different needs or goals and almost certainly has a wider set of educational purposes for schooling, including the education of young people in numerous areas that are not assessed by PISA. Moreover, PISA only assesses 15-year-olds enrolled in school. In some countries, that accounts for little more than half of the population of 15-year-olds.

Point 3: There are right and wrong ways to use PISA.

Technical issues matter and limit how the data can be used. Performance trends should only be evaluated between assessments where the same subject (reading, mathematics, science) is the major domain. Also, the design of PISA is such that students do not answer all of the available items. With this in mind, it is never appropriate to interpret individual or school level scores.

Point 4: The validity of PISA depends on how it is used.

The OECD is not responsible for ensuring the sensible use of PISA data. Only countries can decide if PISA is a valid and reliable test for their given situation. PISA can support systematic inquiry among policy-makers and educators who interrogate the complexities of the data and evaluate the use of PISA data in specific contexts.

Point 5: PISA results do not tell us what to do.

PISA does not measure what is taught in schools. Rather, the assessment focuses on what the OECD believes students should have learned from 15 years of life experience. PISA can show correlations between various school policy settings and the educational performance that it measures, but it cannot show what causes this performance. Ministers and policy-makers must draw on a broad array of information about their schools and societies to develop good policy for their systems.

Point 6: Broader debate could lead to better use of PISA data.

One problem for tests like PISA, and indeed centralized education policy in general, is potential disconnection from life in schools and the expertise of teachers. Unsurprisingly, this can generate resentment and resistance. What we do not see following the release of PISA results is broad consultation about how to interpret the data and what might be done in response. Instead, the tail continues to wag the dog. Many participating governments and ministers are missing opportunities for better data use through engaging with a broader range of perspectives and expertise.

Point 7: PISA envy is toxic.

Being envious of other countries' educational performance involves a strange psychology. It is like an athlete competing against another athlete while desperately wishing to belong to his competitor's team. This is always a futile endeavour. It is much better to focus on your team, accentuate your positives, and try to improve the negatives. Run your own race. The focus on rankings is actually an opportunity for those who could make a difference in educational inequities to avoid their responsibilities. What is your government doing, minister, to improve those social inequalities that schools are not responsible for, but which affect performance as measured by PISA?

If the minister grasps each of these points, then PISA may be one useful tool in a bigger toolbox. Schools and educators should follow the appropriate track for their students rather than rushing to join the global race around the track defined by PISA. We hope this book can contribute to helping policy-makers and educators find the best track for their schools by focusing on the important information, rather than simply rushing to get ahead.

References

Baroutsis, A., & Lingard, B. (2016). Counting and comparing school performance: An analysis of media coverage of PISA in Australia, 2000–2014. *Journal of Education Policy*, 1–18. https://doi.org/10.1080/02680939.2016.1252856

Berliner, D. C. (2015). The many facets of PISA. *Teachers College Record*, *117*(1), 1–20.

Bray, T. M. (2009). Confronting the shadow education system: What government policies for what private tutoring? United Nations Educational, Scientific and Cultural Organization; International Institute for Educational Planning. http://hdl.handle.net/10722/195323

Breakspear, S. (2012). The policy impact of PISA: An exploration of the normative effects of international benchmarking in school system performance. OECD Education Working Papers, No. 71. Paris: OECD Publishing. https://doi.org/10.1787/19939019

Breakspear, S. (2014). How does PISA shape education policy making? Why how we measure learning determines what counts in education. Centre for Strategic Education. Available at: http://simonbreakspear.com/wp-content/uploads/2015/09/Breakspear-PISA-Paper.pdf

Callon, M., Lascoumes, P., & Barthe, Y. (2009). *Acting in an uncertain world: An essay on technical democracy*. Cambridge, MA: MIT Press.

CBC News (2016, December 6). Education minister moves to boost Alberta students' math grades. Retrieved December 7, 2016, from http://www.cbc.ca/news/canada/edmonton/education-minister-moves-to-boost-alberta-students-math-grades-1.3883819

Chan, P. W. K., & Seddon, T. (2014). Governing education in China: PISA, comparison and educational regions. In T. Fenwick, E. Mangez, & J. Ozga (Eds.), *Governing Knowledge. 2014 World Yearbook of Education* (pp. 200–217). UK: Routledge.

Choi, J. (2012, May). Unequal access to shadow education and its impacts on academic outcomes: Evidence from Korea. Paper delivered at the Spring 2012 meeting of ISA RC. 28, 10–13.

Cronbach, L. J. (1980). Validity on parole: How can we go straight? In W. B. Schrader (Ed.). *New directions for testing and measurement: No. 5* (pp. 99–108). San Francisco: Jossey-Bass.

Dohn, B. N. (2007). Knowledge and skills for PISA: Assessing the assessment. *Journal of Philosophy of Education, 41*(1), 1–16. https://doi. org/10.1111/j.1467-9752.2007.00542.x

Feniger, Y., & Lefstein, A. (2014). How not to reason with PISA: An ironic investigation. *Journal of Education Policy, 29*(6), 845–855. https://doi.org/ 10.1080/02680939.2014.892156

Gorur, R., & Wu, M. (2014). Leaning too far? PISA, policy and Australia's "top five" ambitions. *Discourse (Abingdon), 36*(5), 647–664. https://doi.org /10.1080/01596306.2014.930020

Haertel, E. H. (2013). *Reliability and validity of inferences about teachers based on student test scores.* Princeton, NJ: Educational Testing Service.

Henig, J. R. (2013). Foreword. In D. Anagnostopoulos, S. A. Rutledge, & R. Jacobsen (Eds.), *The infrastructure of accountability: Data use and the transformation of American education* (pp. vii–xiii). Cambridge, MA: Harvard Education Press.

Jerrim, J. (2015). Why do East Asian children perform so well in PISA? An investigation of Western-born children of East Asian descent. *Oxford Review of Education, 41*(3), 310–333. https://doi.org/10.1080/03054985.2 015.1028525

Jerrim, J. (2016). PISA 2012: How do the results for the paper and computer tests compare? *Assessment in Education: Principles, Policy & Practice, 23*(4), 495–518. https://doi.org/10.1080/0969594X.2016.1147420

Kane, M. T. (2013). Validation as a pragmatic, scientific activity. *Journal of Educational Measurement, 50*(1), 115–122.

Kane, M. T. (2016). Explicating validity. *Assessment in Education: Principles, Policy & Practice, 23*(2), 198–211. https://doi.org/10.1080/09695 94X.2015.1060192

Klees, S. (2016). Inferences from regression analysis: Are they valid? *Real-world. Economic Review (Kansas City, Mo.), 74,* 85–97. Retrieved from http://www.paecon.net/PAEReview/issue74/Klees74.pdf

Loveless, T. (2014, January 8). PISA's China problem continues: A response to Schleicher, Zhang, and Tucker. Retrieved August 1, 2014, from https://www.brookings.edu/blogs/brown-center-chalkboard/ posts/2014/01/08-shanghai-pisa-loveless

Maddox, B. (2014). Globalising assessment: An ethnography of literacy assessment, camels and fast food in the Mongolian Gobi. *Comparative Education, 50*(4), 474–489. https://doi.org/10.1080/03050068.2013.871440

Messick, S. (1987). Validity. *ETS Research Report Series*, i–208.

Norwegian Directorate for Education and Training (2011). *OECD review on evaluation and assessment frameworks for improving school outcomes: Country background report for Norway* (p. 115). Norway. Retrieved from https://www.udir.no/Upload/Rapporter/2011/5/OECD_country_report_norway.pdf?epslanguage=no

OECD (2010). *Making reform happen: Lessons from OECD countries*. Paris: OECD Publishing.

OECD (2012). *PISA 2009 Technical Report*. Paris: OECD Publishing. Retrieved from http://www.oecd.org/edu/preschoolandschool/programmeforinternationalstudentassessmentpisa/pisa2009technicalreport.htm

OECD (2014). *PISA 2012 technical report*. Paris: OECD Publishing.

OECD (2016a). PISA 2015 assessment and analytical framework. Paris: Organisation for Economic Co-operation and Development. Retrieved from http://www.oecd-ilibrary.org/content/book/9789264255425-en

OECD (2016b). Ten questions for mathematics teachers…and how PISA can help answer them. Paris: OECD Publishing. Available online: http://www.oecd.org/edu/ten-questions-for-mathematics-teachers-and-how-pisa-can-help-answer-them-9789264265387-en.htm

OECD (2016c). *PISA 2015 results: Excellence and equity in education* (Vol. 1). Paris: OECD Publishing.

Rutkowski, D., & Rutkowski, L. (2013). Measuring socioeconomic background in PISA: One size might not fit all. *Research in Comparative and International Education, 8*(3), 259–278. https://doi.org/10.2304/rcie.2013.8.3.259

Rutkowski, L., & Rutkowski, D. (2016). A call for a more measured approach to reporting and interpreting PISA results. *Educational Researcher, 45*(4), 252–257. https://doi.org/10.3102/0013189X16649961

Sahlberg, P. (2015). *Finnish lessons 2.0: What can the world learn from educational change in Finland?* (2nd ed.). New York: Teachers College Press.

Steiner-Khamsi, G. (2003). The politics of league tables. *Journal of Social Science Education. Online (Bergheim)*. https://doi.org/10.4119/UNIBI/jsse-v2-i1-470

The Local (2016, December 6). Norwegian teens over the hump in global school rankings. Retrieved December 7, 2016, from http://www.thelocal.no/20161206/norwegian-teens-over-the-hump-in-global-school-rankings

Waldow, F. (2017). Projecting images of the "good" and the "bad" school:
Top scorers in educational large-scale assessments as reference societies.
Compare: A Journal of Comparative Education, 1–18. Retrieved from
https://doi.org/10.1080/03057925.2016.1262245

Waldow, F., Takayama, K., & Sung, Y.-K. (2014). Rethinking the pattern of
external policy referencing: Media discourses over the "Asian Tigers" PISA
success in Australia, Germany and South Korea. *Comparative Education*,
50(3), 302–321. https://doi.org/10.1080/03050068.2013.860704

Whatmore, S. J., & Landstrom, C. (2011). Flood apprentices: An exercise in
making things public. *Economy and Society*, *40*(4), 582–610. https://doi.
org/10.1080/03085147.2011.602540

About the Authors

Sam Sellar is Reader in Education Studies at Manchester Metropolitan University and a director of the Laboratory of International Assessment Studies. He was previously Postdoctoral Senior Research Fellow in the School of Education at the University of Queensland. Sam has studied school systems in Australia, Canada, and the United Kingdom to explore how educational data shape policy and practice in schools. He has published widely on the growing influence of data in education globally, including the education work of the OECD and its Programme for International Student Assessment. Sam was formerly an editor of the journal *Critical Studies in Education* and is currently an associate editor of *Discourse: Studies in the Cultural Politics of Education*.

Greg Thompson is Associate Professor of Education Research at Queensland University of Technology (QUT). Prior to becoming an academic, he worked as a high school teacher in Western Australia for 13 years. He graduated with a PhD from Murdoch University, where he worked from 2010–2015 in the School of Education before taking up his position at QUT in July 2015. From 2012–2015, Thompson was an Australian Research Council Fellow examining the

effects of Australia's national testing regime (NAPLAN) on
school communities. Thompson's research interests focus
on educational theory, education policy, and the philoso-
phy/sociology of education assessment and measurement,
with a particular emphasis on large-scale testing. Recent
research projects include reconceptualizing test validity,
instructional rounds as professional learning, education
policy and teachers' perceptions of time, decision making with data, and the impending impact of learning ana-
lytics/Big Data on schools. He is the Australasian editor
of the *Journal of Education Policy* and associate editor of
Discourse: Studies in the Cultural Politics of Education. He is
also series editor of two book series, *Local/Global Issues in
Education* (Routledge) and *Deleuze and Education Research*
(Edinburgh University Press).

David Rutkowski is Professor of Education at the Center
for Educational Measurement at the University of
Oslo, Norway. He was previously a faculty member at
Indiana University and also worked as a researcher at the
International Association for the Evaluation of Educational
Achievement (IEA) in Hamburg, Germany. He earned his
PhD in educational policy from the University of Illinois at
Urbana-Champaign. David's research is focused in the area
of educational policy and technical topics within international large-scale assessment. He has published numerous
peer-reviewed articles, was co-editor of the *Handbook of
International Large-Scale Assessment*, serves on a number
of journal editorial boards, and is editor of the IEA policy
brief series. David has collaborated with or consulted for
numerous national and international organizations, including the US State Department, USAID, the IEA, and the
OECD. David has worked on evaluations and projects in
over 20 countries, including Afghanistan, South Sudan,
Trinidad and Tobago, and the United States.